Let Ever␣ Prepare Him Room

Advent Reflections

by Ted Wueste

Published by Desert Direction, Phoenix, AZ

Library of Congress Cataloguing-in-Publication Data
Wueste, Ted
Let Every Heart Prepare Him Room: Advent Reflections / Ted Wueste
Library of Congress Control Number: 2015949669

    ISBN 9781515380733
           1. Devotional. 2. Advent. 3. Spiritual Formation.

Printed in the United States of America
First Edition

CONTENTS

ACKNOWLEDGMENTS

Thanks to all those who encouraged the publication of this Advent Devotional. I am also very thankful to those who helped with editing and suggestions: Michael Donnelly, Toni Donnelly, and Ann Kelly. Thanks to Courtney Larson who developed the cover art and design.

Thanks to my church family at Bethany Bible Church with whom I get to serve in His kingdom.

And, I am beyond thankful to my bride, Jenifer, and amazing kids, Trey and Claire, who were supportive through long nights and early mornings of writing and rewriting. Often, you didn't know exactly what I was up to but you trusted. I love you three so much.

INTRODUCTION

The word "advent" comes from a Latin word ("adventus") which means "coming." Traditionally, the church has taken the weeks leading up to Christmas to "live into" the story of waiting for Messiah to appear. Advent is a season that reminds us of our longing and desire.

Advent is a time of waiting. A line from the Christmas hymn, *Joy to the World*, says it so well: "Let every heart prepare him room." During these days of Advent, we are challenged to consider that part of the waiting is preparing … preparing room in our hearts to experience anew the One true object of our longing and desire.

In the midst of the busyness of the season, slow down and prepare room in your heart. Over the next four weeks, we'll walk through four movements related to preparing room in our hearts as we listen to His voice.

How will you listen this Advent season?

PREPARATION

Let Every Heart Prepare Him Room

On Christmas, we sing *Joy to the World* with the phrase, "let every heart prepare Him room." Quite often, these are simply sentimental words. They are words we like and words we want to be true. However, preparation takes time and we can't wish our way into preparing room for God in our lives.

In our world of "instant everything", we can easily transfer the idea of "instant" into our lives with God. We desire to be able to "say the word" and experience relationship with Him. On the one hand, He is always present in our lives but often not in an experiential way. We might "know" that He is near but not experience that nearness in the daily moments of life. The invitation to "prepare Him room" is an invitation to experience Him at the heart level, at the level of our conscious awareness and not simply at the level of theological assent. This doesn't happen in an instant … it requires preparation in the same way we might prepare to have a house guest.

For many of us, our hearts are like the homes on the television show *Hoarders*. Every square inch of our hearts is filled with things that we believe will make us happy: relationships, jobs, activities, possessions, even "religious" activities. None of these is "bad", but they aren't meant to satisfy our souls. And then, we frequently hold hurts, grudges, habits, or other desires in our hearts. Throw in the busyness of life and there just isn't any room for a visitor.

On *Hoarders*, the cleaning project begins with a humble acknowledgement that there is a need for change. Over these next three and a half weeks of Advent, we'll walk through a process for making room in our hearts for Christ.

Our life with God is always an adventure in what Eugene Peterson calls the "middle voice". In the English language, we understand "active voice" in which we do something and the "passive voice" in which something is done to us. Other languages have the "middle voice" in which one is active and passive at the same time. Peterson writes:

> Prayer and spirituality feature participation, the complex participation of God and the human, his will and our wills. We do not abandon ourselves to drown in the ocean of love, losing identity. We do not pull the strings that activate God's operations in our lives, subjecting God to our assertive identity. We neither manipulate God (active voice) nor are we manipulated by God (passive voice). We are involved in the action and participate in its results but do not control or define it (middle voice). Prayer takes place in the middle voice.

The middle voice means that we wait ... actively, and that is what advent is all about. There is tension in the waiting but there is no other way. So, the idea is that we allow Him to prepare room in our hearts but we also participate. How will this work? As we allow Him

4

to prepare the room, what is our role? Over these next weeks of the Advent Season, we'll walk through the following:

Week 1: He humbles our hearts as we *wait*

Week 2: He softens our hearts as we *listen*

Week 3: He expands our hearts as we *release*

Week 4: He occupies our hearts as we *open*

Let's journey together in these days of Advent as we learn to wait, listen, release, open, and finally celebrate the one who comes to live in our hearts!

Advent comes from a Latin word which means "coming" or "arrival" and the days of Advent challenge us to prepare and be in waiting mode. We may have come to know Jesus years ago, but Advent once again allows us to go deeper into the joy of a Savior who dwells with us and in us. He alone is the One for whom we were made. It was Augustine who prayed, "Our heart is restless until it rests in you." Let's pray his prayer as we begin living into this Season of Advent …

> *Great are you, O Lord, and exceedingly worthy of praise; your power is immense, and your wisdom beyond reckoning. And so we, who are a due part of your creation, long to praise you — we also carry our mortality about with us, carry the evidence of our sin and with it the proof that you thwart the proud. You arouse us so that praising you may bring us joy, because you have made us and drawn us to yourself, and our heart is restless until it rests in you. Amen.*

Spend some time with that prayer and make it your own.

Tomorrow, we begin with learning to wait ... that He might humble our heart

DECEMBER 1

He Humbles Our Hearts as We Wait
Day 1

The preparation of our hearts begins with waiting. Waiting? That dreaded word! We don't like to wait. Why? Because waiting humbles us … it reminds us that we aren't in control … that we can't save ourselves. It puts us in a place of depending on someone else. We don't like it because it strips us down to simply "being" rather than "doing." Most of our "doing" is about clothing ourselves so we don't have to feel naked and vulnerable. Our "doings" are generally an attempt to clothe ourselves with relationships, possessions, or achievements.

To just "be" feels vulnerable, but it is in our vulnerability that He meets us. It is not in our attempts to control things that we experience Him but in our weakness and dependence. When we feel vulnerable, with a lack of security or power or respect, we try to make things happen. We try to save ourselves. And that is our undoing …

It is when we wait that a Savior can appear. When we strike out on our own, we never sense our need and never cry out for help. We might ask him to help us save ourselves but He desires to save us into life with Him, being clothed in Him, not saving us with the clothes we think we want.

Initially, when we come to faith, it is because we stopped and believed that we couldn't save ourselves. Then, day by day, we experience His salvation in our lives when we wait for Him to keep on saving us.

In Psalm 25:1-3, David cries out to God:

> To You, O Lord, I lift up my soul. O my God, in You I trust, Do not let me be ashamed; Do not let my enemies exult over me. Indeed, none of those who wait for You will be ashamed; Those who deal treacherously without cause will be ashamed. (NASB)

Why does he pray "do not let me be ashamed"? Because David was face to face with his need, his nakedness. He knew he needed to be clothed. He expresses the faith of waiting, knowing that God will clothe Him. Those who "deal treacherously" speaks of those times when we take matters into our own hands. David affirms that this always leads to shame because we simply can't clothe ourselves adequately. We are always left with incompleteness.

When we wait, we experience the God who has always been there. It requires stopping and waiting to notice what has been ours all along. When we wait, we become aware ... aware of the ways we try to save ourselves and aware of the Savior who is always with us.

Make it a goal to wait today. When you feel that urge to take control of a situation, stop and wait for your Savior. Feel that sense of nakedness but let it be an invitation to trust, not action.

We'll pray this prayer together throughout this week of asking the Father to humble our hearts as we wait:

Gracious Father, humble my heart as I wait on you. Give me the strength to stop and wait so that you can be the One who saves me. Give me eyes to see my nakedness today but then to trust that You alone can clothe me. Use your Word, the world around me, and the words of others that I might see You alone as my savior all the day long. Amen.

DECEMBER 2

He Humbles Our Hearts as We Wait
Day 2

Preparing room in our hearts for Jesus *begins* as He humbles our hearts through waiting. We wait when we embrace the mystery that is the work of God in our lives. There is a deep mystery to the ways of our Father. There is a sublime simplicity to the incarnation and also a mystery to its application in our lives. To put it another way, theologians have noticed that there is an "already/not yet" to the Gospel of Jesus. For us today, it is "already" true that God the Son was born into a manger and died for our sins. There is deep joy in this reality, and there is also a "not yet" to experiencing all the ramifications of forgiveness and new life.

In 1 John 3:2-3, John expresses this "already/not yet" reality:

> Beloved, we are God's children now, and what we will be has not yet appeared; but we know that when he appears we shall be like him, because we shall see him as he is. And everyone who thus hopes in him purifies himself as he is pure.

Living in between the "already" and the "not yet" requires waiting, but it is not a passive waiting. It is, in John's words, a purifying waiting based in hope. Waiting means that we hold tight to a God who has more in store than we are presently experiencing. Rather than try to understand and control the transitions between now and then, we wait in the hope that a process is unfolding. The end of the process is described in terms of his second appearing and we live in between the two appearings. As we wait for our ultimate salvation, we experience tastes and touches of His love ("what we will be has not yet appeared"), but they are only tastes.

We are purified when we live in the tension ... the tension of the mystery. We don't have all the answers ... there is much that has not yet appeared. Not knowing can create frustration or even result in acting impulsively, but a hopeful waiting purifies. Purity is the result because we live in dependence upon Him and not the independence of self-provision.

Pierre Teilhard de Chardin encourages:

> Above all else, trust the slow work of God. We are quite naturally impatient in everything to reach the end without delay. We should like to skip the intermediate stages. We are impatient of being on the way to something unknown, something new. Only God could say what this new spirit gradually forming in you will be. Give our Lord the benefit that His hand is leading you, and accept the anxiety of feeling yourself in suspense, and incomplete.

As the people of Israel journeyed to the land which would flow with milk and honey, God gave them daily bread ("the manna"). It was enough for the day but it was not the milk and honey. It was given with the hope that something more was coming. The people of Israel were frustrated and acted out. We can be short-sighted and judge the transitions as though they were the final answer. Waiting sees the tensions and incompleteness, enjoying the tastes and touches in light of something more.

Notice those places and times today when you feel incomplete and in suspense, desiring more. Rather than try to get rid of the mystery, embrace it and wait with hope … the hope of a Savior who is going to appear.

Pray this prayer again through the day as you receive His invitation to wait …

Gracious Father, humble my heart as I wait on you. Give me the strength to stop and wait so that you can be the One who saves me. Give me eyes to see my nakedness today but then to trust that You alone can clothe me. Use your Word, the world around me, and the words of others that I might see You alone as my savior all the day long. Amen.

He Humbles Our Hearts as We Wait
Day 3

Singing the song "Silent Night" at this time of year can be a deeply moving experience. The very use of the words "silent" and "holy" to describe a singular evening, draw us into the sacred drama of God the Son entering human history. There is something about the holiness of the moment that silences us. When we encounter the holy, there are not words that can adequately describe. Silence ends up being the perfect language.

Indeed, silence has been called the first language of God. In 1 Kings 19, it was the "sound of silence" which elicited awe and humility from Elijah's heart. Silence takes away the pretense that noise often affords our hearts. When things are noisy, we can hide and pretend behind the clamor and the clanging. Our explanations and defenses are laid down in the arena of silence, leaving us in the purity of just being before a good and gracious Savior. It can be scary but it is purifying and full of awe.

A moment of silence on Christmas Eve is beautiful but a regular practice of silence ushers us into a way of living that transcends circumstance and makes us aware of the holy all around. The response to a holy moment is silence, but equally true is that silence can give us eyes to see the holy.

As we consider learning to wait in order to humble our hearts, silence plays a huge part. In Psalm 65, King David cries out, "For God alone my soul waits in silence. For God alone, O my soul, wait in silence, for my hope is from him."

Robert L'Esperance, one of the brothers of the Society of St. John the Evangelist said:

> Advent is a time to look for 'desert places': the place of solitude, the place of true silence in which we can become fully awake to our sin and God's forgiving grace which alone can heal it.

Take 5-10 minutes today to be quiet. Sit in silence and just listen. Quietly repeat the words of Psalm 65: "For God alone my soul waits in silence." Then, wait quietly. As thoughts or distractions rush in, simply pray the words of Psalm 65.

There is nothing magic about "practicing" silence but it does express a deep trust in God that goes deeper than words. It touches the depths of our being because it goes past the surface noise of life.

Finally, once again pray this simple prayer of waiting throughout the day today:

> *Gracious Father, humble my heart as I wait on you. Give me the strength to stop and wait so that you can be the One who saves me. Give me eyes to see my nakedness today but then to trust that You alone can clothe me. Use your Word, the world around me, and the words of others that I might see You alone as my savior all the day long. Amen.*

He Humbles Our Hearts as We Wait
Day 4

The receiving and giving of gifts is inextricably linked to the Christmas season, and Advent is a time of learning to wait for the good gifts of Christmas. Children often make the season about getting and having as they impatiently obsess about what gifts they will receive and how soon they can be opened. The mature, however, understand that gifts are always about relationship, trusting in the nature and timing of the gifts to be received.

The discipline of waiting prepares our hearts to receive the good gifts that God gives us. When we are impatient, we are looking at life and God on our own terms … seeking to meet our needs according to our definitions and our timing. Waiting slows us down and humbles us, reminding us that the true gift is the giver Himself … One who loves us deeply. When our focus becomes the giver, we are able to receive His provision not as a deserved right but as a gracious gift that perfectly suits us.

When we are suffering or in need, we often clamor and complain, but God's counsel is that we become "quick to hear, slow to speak, slow to anger." (James 1:19) Why?

Because "every good gift and every perfect gift is from above, coming down from the Father of lights with whom there is no variation or shadow due to change." (James 1:17) He always gives and provides exactly what we need and frequently there is a waiting period. Waiting creates a humility in our hearts that gives us fresh eyes to see His gifts that have often been present all along.

We think we want miracles and change and action but what we desire in the depths of our hearts is Him. He will let us wait so that we have the best opportunity to see and appreciate Him as our gift.

One of the challenges in our world today is that we don't have to wait. We can use a credit card to buy our way out of a tough situation. We can get a new job and move on to escape suffering. We can jump on a plane and be on the beach in an hour. The list could go on, but the reality is, all too often we simply don't wait for the good gifts that He brings.

Again, what are His gifts? In Luke 11:1-13, Jesus asks several questions to lead us into understanding how He works:

> What father among you, if his son asks for a fish, will instead of a fish give him a serpent; or if he asks for an egg, will give him a scorpion? If you then, who are evil, know how to give good gifts to your children, how much more will the heavenly Father give the Holy Spirit to those who ask him!

We seek and ask for a specific kind of provision and He not only gives but gives better than we even know how to ask. And, again, the gift is His presence in the Holy Spirit. In Psalm 40, David cries out:

"I waited patiently for the LORD; He inclined to me and heard my cry." David waited and realized that the Lord "inclined and heard" … He was present.

Do you trust that **His presence** is the gift above all gifts? Better than life itself? Waiting only makes sense in light of this reality, and learning to wait opens our heart to this gift above all gifts. And, the beauty is that we experience this gift in our waiting and then are able to receive anything else as a function of relationship, not rights. Our expectations change. Our prayers change. We change …

John Ortberg states:

> What always drives us, at the soul level, is that if I believe I cannot trust God for the satisfaction of my soul, then I will take my soul's satisfaction into my own hands. I may not acknowledge that even to myself.

Today, look for the gift of His presence in your life. Set an alarm on your phone, watch or computer for several times throughout the day. When the alarm goes off, stop and ask, "How am I seeing the gift of His presence today?" Ponder, acknowledge, thank Him, and then pray the following:

> *Gracious Father, humble my heart as I wait on you. Give me the strength to stop and wait so that you can be the One who saves me. Give me eyes to see my nakedness today but then to trust that You alone can clothe me. Use your Word, the world around me, and the words of others that I might see You alone as my savior all the day long. Amen.*

He Humbles Our Hearts as We Wait
Day 5

Waiting can be wearying if we are simply waiting as an exercise of our will power. However, the Biblical concept of waiting is not a "grit your teeth and bear it" kind of thing. It's a joyful resting in the goodness and grace of God. We might not see His goodness and grace in our present circumstances, but this restful waiting unlocks the deep truth that He is always at work and He is always present in our lives.

Author Paula Gooder encourages the spiritual discipline of waiting as she writes:

> Waiting draws us into a different way of being that does not rush to easy answers — that often have complex consequences — but takes account of not just our own welfare but that of all those around us. Waiting involves seeing differently and recognizing that quick answers are not always the best ones.

The answers that we can rush into often work at a subconscious level. When we can't see God at work, deep in our heart we may assume that He isn't at work. Consequently, we feel this urge to take charge. Our world is rife with "wisdom" that we have to take charge and seize the opportunity. That narrative seeps into our souls. The result is that we put ourselves in the driver's seat and reduce God to a kindly repairman who will keep our car running.

Thankfully, God is patient with us and He has bigger plans for us. He desires for us to live in a trustful rhythm where He is in the driver's seat and we are His servants, His friends. Waiting humbles us and reminds us of our created design which is also our greatest joy.

In the New Testament Epistle of James, we read the challenging counsel:

> Be patient, therefore, brothers, until the coming of the Lord.
> See how the farmer waits for the precious fruit of the earth,
> being patient about it, until it receives the early and the late
> rains. You also, be patient. Establish your hearts, for the
> coming of the Lord is at hand.
> James 5:7-8

The challenge? Be patient … wait. The context of this challenge is looking at the "rich" who use their wealth for themselves. We may not, by definition, be rich but there is an attitude of self … self-preservation, self-promotion, self-protection … that can be a part of our lives. The lie is that we can or even should be the master of our world. To that attitude, the counsel is: be patient. Why? Because when life seems out of control (i.e., "Where is God? Does He even care? Is He involved here?"), our temptation is to seize the wheel. The counsel? Be patient. Wait. Why? Two reasons:

1. The coming of the Lord is at hand (or near). The idea is that He is involved. **He is present.** He does have a plan. So, be patient ...

2. **He is at work.** The "early and late rains" reference is often lost on a modern audience. The early and late rains are symbols of God's provision and a farmer's dependence upon something outside himself to take care of things. The people of Israel were geographically and meteorologically dependent as they raised crops. In contrast, Egyptian farmers (and the people of Israel experienced this as slaves in Egypt) built irrigation canals. They used water from the Nile and other rivers anytime they desired. They were in control. God's counsel here is that we can be patient because He is in charge and we can trust Him. He will provide.

Why depend upon God if we have our own resources? Because dependence on God is indeed our created design and only waiting will usher us into a place of dependence.

The "established heart" in James 5 is a strong heart which is humble because it is shaped by hope in God — not hope in self. Having our own resources and trusting in them creates the illusion that we are strong. The deep truth is that this makes us weak because it creates stress in us and converts us into that we were never designed to be, independent beings who are disconnected from God.

Spend a few minutes with the Lord, asking Him, *In what ways am I like a "rich" farmer? How am I tempted to build my own irrigation ditches rather than trust that You are present and at work?*

Finally, express your trust and dependence as you pray:

> *Gracious Father, humble my heart as I wait on you. Give me the strength to stop and wait so that you can be the One who saves me. Give me eyes to see my nakedness today but then to trust that You alone can clothe me. Use your Word, the world around me, and the words of others that I might see You alone as my savior all the day long. Amen.*

Note: tomorrow we look at "waiting" for another day and then move into "preparing room" - the amazing truth that *He softens our hearts as we listen.*

He Humbles Our Hearts as We Wait
Day 6

The great German pastor Dietrich Bonhoeffer said that "the celebration of Advent is possible only to those who are troubled in soul, who know themselves to be poor and imperfect, and who look forward to something greater to come."

This may sound strange to our modern ears but it actually contains the echoes of the eternal, timeless message of Jesus when He said in Matthew 5:3: "Blessed are the poor in spirit for theirs is the kingdom of God." It is the humble who know they need a Savior moment by moment in life. And, it is the humble who experience blessing because they are living under His gracious rule in their lives ("kingdom of God").

The harsh reality is that living with a sense that we are poor and imperfect doesn't come naturally or easily. We are much more likely to adopt another, much more self-protective, response to life in a broken, mixed up world. There are generally two paths:

First, **we might be complainers**. We might not think of ourselves as complainers but do you ever believe that if only situations and people changed, you could be happy? Do you ever consider the difficulties in your life to simply be the fault of others?

Here's the problem: when we complain, we are keeping difficult things at a distance rather than embracing the reality that we are being affected. Instead of looking inward at how we are responding to life, we are pushing everything away from us. Complaining keeps us distanced from reality and therefore from God. God lives in the reality of what is, not in our conceptions of the way we wish things were.

Second, **we might be in denial**. This is the polar opposite of being a complainer but with the same effect. Those in denial act like everything is "just fine" even when it isn't. There are times and situations that are just plain hard. Like complaining, when we live in denial, we are also not embracing reality.

There is, however, a third way and it is in the middle of these two extremes. It is the way of James 1:19 where we are challenged to be "quick to listen, slow to speak, and slow to anger."

1. Being "quick to listen" means that **we stop and ask God** about what is going on. Rather than complaining (assuming we know how to assess things) or living in denial (acting like everything is really ok), we humble ourselves by asking, "God, what do you want to say about what's going on?"

2. Being "slow to speak" means that **we stay in a place of dependence upon God**. What will be has not yet been revealed. What His plans are for this situation have not completely played out. We wait rather than spew our incomplete perspective.

3. Being "slow to anger" means that **we consider the deeper emotions underlying our response**. Anger is a secondary emotion. There is always something deeper going on that results in anger. Perhaps it is hurt or embarrassment or disappointment or shame or fear. There may be times where anger is appropriate, but only when it is not covering a deeper emotion. Anger that is used to cover deeper emotion can be unwieldy and damaging to us and others.

When we stop, stay, and consider, the result is that we are waiting with God and not rushing away from pain. We are able to confront our own poverty and imperfection. As a result, we live with a **contentment** that God is with us and He is at work. G. K. Chesterton wrote that contentment is "the power of getting out of a situation all that there is in it."

Andreas Ebert suggested much the same:

> If we are unwilling to live askew for a while, to be set off balance, to wait on the ever spacious threshold, we remain in the same old room all our lives. If we will not balance knowing with a kind of open-ended *not knowing* - nothing seems to happen. Thus it is called 'faith' and demands living with a certain degree of anxiety and holding a very real amount of tension.

The counsel to slow down and wait, places us in a perfect position to listen to God and sets us up for the next movement in our journey of "preparing Him room in our hearts."

Today, as you encounter the hard things of life (whether things close to home or things you're seeing in the news), ask yourself, *Do I tend to complain or live in denial?* Notice your tendencies, but move away from them.

Ask God what He has to say - wait for His wisdom before you speak.

Consider what is going on in your heart - deeper than the anger.

Stay in a place of waiting dependence - once again, pray this prayer:

> *Gracious Father, humble my heart as I wait on you. Give me the strength to stop and wait so that you can be the One who saves me. Give me eyes to see my nakedness today but then to trust that You alone can clothe me. Use your Word, the world around me, and the words of others that I might see You alone as my savior all the day long. Amen.*

DECEMBER 7

He Softens Our Hearts as We Listen
Day 1

There is a difference between hearing and listening. Hearing is when we are able to physically register that there is a sound in our environment. Hearing may even extend to translating those sounds into some sort of meaning. Listening, however, occurs when we take those words to heart.

In Hebrews 3:7-8, there is a phrase that is repeated several times in the chapter, "Today, if you hear His voice, don't harden your hearts." In these words, we see the difference between and the importance of hearing and listening. Hearing speaks of the content ("if you hear His voice") and listening has to do with the heart ("don't harden your hearts"). As we choose to listen, God softens our hearts. When we don't listen, our hearts are hard or resistant to what God is saying.

Note of caution: we generally would not consider ourselves to be hard of heart. However, hardness of heart - or not listening to God - is seen in the Scriptures as a real challenge. Over and over, God implores us to look at our hearts.

Those who are committed and serious about God may tend to have all the right actions, but they are not from the heart (cf. Matthew

23:25-26, the outside of the cup is clean but the inside is full of greed and self-indulgence). Others may initially receive what is said but fail to listen amid the clamor and noise of life (cf. Mark 4:16-17, the troubles of life are a distraction). Finally, there are some who are distracted because other desires seem to be stronger (cf. Mark 4:18-19, the promise of riches and others things to make life easy).

There is **something deeper** than the *pride* of right actions and the *hurts* of harsh realities and the *desires* for a pain-free existence. That something deeper is what is promised at Christmas: a life with God … a life where we are experiencing love, joy, peace, patience, goodness, because we are experiencing Him and listening to Him.

To receive the gifts of Christmas, we have to be able to listen. We don't change and grow through magic or wishing it so, but through a relationship of listening (heartfelt response to what is heard; often called "obedience"). We begin relationship with God through receiving the gift of forgiveness because of what Jesus did on the cross. We grow in the relationship as we do what He asks. His "asks" for our hearts - all the commands of Scripture are for our hearts - that we would live from the heart according to our created design.

We need to be able to hear … and listen.

We spent the first week of Advent learning to wait … letting go of our perspectives, interpretations, and expectations. In doing this, He humbles us so that we are now in a place of being able to listen.

As we embark on sharpening our listening skills, there is one thing we need to keep in mind. He is always speaking. Several hundred years ago, Francois Fenelon wrote,

> We must silence every creature, including self, that in the deep stillness of soul we may perceive the ineffable voice of the Bridegroom. We must lend an attentive ear, for his voice is soft and still, and is only heard by those who hear nothing else! Ah, how rare it is to find a soul still enough to hear God speak! The slightest murmur of our vain desires, or of a love fixed upon self, confounds all the words of the Spirit of God. We hear well enough that he is speaking, and that he is asking for something, but we cannot distinguish what is said … let us recognize, then, the fact that God is incessantly speaking in us.

As we begin this week of listening, practice a simple discipline today. Take 5-10 minutes of solitude and ask: "Father, what you do desire to say to me today?"

Begin with this Scripture:

> Therefore, as the Holy Spirit says, "Today, if you hear his voice, do not harden your hearts as in the rebellion, on the day of testing in the wilderness. (Hebrews 3:7-8)

Sit quietly and listen. Are there are voices, noises, or thoughts distracting you? Don't try to control the distractions, just let them go (this is part of learning to hear/listen) and return to listening with a simple, "Father, your servant is listening." Don't worry if you don't hear anything, you are simply learning to put yourself in a place to hear/listen.

At the end of this time, simply pray:

Father, help me to silence every creature, including myself. I want to listen to You as I hear your voice. Help me to learn stillness so that I might be attentive to Your good and gracious voice. As I hear, may I have the courage to follow Your heart from my heart. Thank you for desiring to do life with me.

DECEMBER 8

He Softens Our Hearts as We Listen Day 2

We can often catch ourselves saying, "I just wish God would speak to me!" He has and He does. He is always speaking (even through His silence) and He is always at work (just not in ways that we might expect). Christmas is a grand testimony to the voice and activity of God, and yet it is easy to miss Him in the commotion of the season.

Humility is foundational to listening because we must let go of our own perspectives and prejudices. Seeing through the lens of our perspective and prejudice will cloud our ability to see God at work.

Thomas Merton, author and Trappist monk, commented that there is a difference between looking and seeing.

> When we look, we have something in mind that we want to see. We've made up our mind about what we believe we need and only look for it. When we see, we are open to whatever it is that God brings before us. There is an openness and receptivity. Humility allows us to see rather than simply look, and consequently, we are able to see (listen to) God.

In Hebrews 3, God says, "If you hear my voice, don't harden your heart" and the following verses describe a dynamic where God was speaking but people didn't hear:

...do not harden your hearts as in the rebellion, on the day of testing in the wilderness, where your fathers put me to the test and saw my works for forty years. Therefore I was provoked with that generation, and said, 'They always go astray in their heart; they have not known my ways.' (3:8-10)

The writer of Hebrews is describing the people's inability to listen to what God had been saying for all those years. What were the works that they saw for forty years? It began with being delivered from slavery in Egypt and the parting of the Red Sea. He miraculously provided water and daily bread. Even as they complained, He provided quail to eat. The list could go on, but it can definitely be said that God was at work! They could perceive (hear) but they didn't get it (listen). It was an issue of the heart ("they always go astray in their heart") that led to not knowing His ways.

In Isaiah 55:8, God says, "For my thoughts are not your thoughts, neither are your ways my ways." This seems obvious enough but is there a reliable way forward? In the previous verses, God shares the foundation of this difference:

Come, everyone who thirsts, come to the waters; and he who has no money, come, buy and eat! Come, buy wine and milk without money and without price. Why do you spend your money for that which is not bread, and your labor for that which does not satisfy? Listen diligently to me, and eat what is good, and delight yourselves in rich food. Incline your ear and come to me; hear, that your soul may live. (Is. 55:1-3)

The water and the bread in these verses are God Himself.

Relationship with Him is a gift ("without money and without price") and is the only thing which will satisfy us. These words provoke questions: *do I thirst and hunger for God? Or, am I hungry for that which does not satisfy?* Our desires shape our hearts and consequently our ability to listen. I see what I desire. I hear what I want. The way that we hear God is by desiring Him. If I am seeking God but "listening" in a different language (desiring things other than Him), I will miss it when He is speaking. It would be like listening to the radio in a language not our own. We hear things but they don't translate.

Set aside some time for quiet prayer and ask God to show you what you most desire. Likely, there is a mixture of things (some pure and some impure). Get a blank piece of paper and a pen. Ask Him to help you see those places in your heart where you desire to find satisfaction in things other than Him. As the Father brings things to your mind, write them down. Finally, mentally walk through each thing and cross it out as you simply pray, "Father, I desire you more than this."

End your time with this prayer of listening:

> *Father, help me to silence every creature, including myself. I want to listen to You as I hear your voice. Help me to learn stillness so that I might be attentive to Your good and gracious voice. As I hear, may I have the courage to follow Your heart from my heart. Thank you for desiring to do life with me.*

DECEMBER 9

He Softens Our Hearts As We Listen
Day 3

There is something about the Advent and Christmas Season that gives us an expectation of hearing from God. Maybe it comes from some of the songs we sing like, "Do You Hear What I Hear?" Perhaps, it is something even deeper that is stirred this time of year.

Ecclesiastes 3:11 says, "He has made everything beautiful in its time. Also, he has put eternity into man's heart, yet so that he cannot find out what God has done from the beginning to the end." There are seasons to life (described in the previous verses) ... all of which are beautiful, purposeful, and meaningful as we listen to God. The idea of "eternity in the heart" is that we intuitively have a sense that life is much bigger than us. However, the phrase "he cannot find out" speaks to the reality that we are finite creatures and need God's voice to speak into the circumstances of our lives.

The words from Hebrews 3 that encourage, "If you hear His voice, don't harden your heart," are part of a quote from Psalm 95. In the verses prior this encouragement to listen, we find this challenge, "Let us come into his presence with thanksgiving." (Psalm 95:2)

The idea is simple. Because God is infinite and omnipresent, we are always in His presence. However, there is the *truth* of His presence and there is the *experience* of His presence. The psalmist is declaring that we come into, or experience, His presence when we are thankful. Gratefulness gives us ears to hear God. Psalm 100:4 declares the same idea with slightly different words, "Enter his gates with thanksgiving, and his courts with praise!"

A thankful heart enables us to hear what God is saying through all the events and circumstances of our lives. The verse in Ecclesiastes about everything being beautiful in its time refers to the familiar verses preceding it in Ecclesiastes 3:1-8:

> For everything there is a season,
>
> and time for every matter under heaven:
>
> a time to be born, and a time to die;
>
> a time to plant, and a time to pluck up what is planted;
>
> a time to kill, and a time to heal;
>
> a time to break down, and a time to build up;
>
> a time to weep, and a time to laugh;
>
> a time to mourn, and a time to dance;
>
> a time to cast away stones, and
>
> a time to gather stones together;
>
> a time to embrace, and a time to refrain from embracing;
>
> a time to seek, and a time to lose;
>
> a time to keep, and a time to cast away;
>
> a time to tear, and a time to sew;
>
> a time to keep silence, and a time to speak;
>
> a time to love, and a time to hate;
>
> a time for war, and a time for peace."

How are we able to be thankful in all of these things? It is rooted in the trust that He is present with us in all things. He is speaking.

In his book, *Everything Belongs,* Richard Rohr said, "Everything belongs and everything can be received. We don't have to deny, dismiss, defy, or ignore. What is, is okay. What is, is the great teacher. I have always seen this as the deep significance of Jesus' refusal of the drugged wine on the cross."

When we approach everything in life as an opportunity for God to speak to us and teach us and lead us, we are in a place to hear from Him. When we are thankful, we move into a place to listen. When we are *not* thankful, we might be able to conceptually understand that God is at work in all things but we will likely not be open to what He has to say. We will likely not be able to receive each circumstance as Him speaking to us.

The opposite of gratitude is not ingratitude, but entitlement. In each situation of life, we either approach it with gratitude (God is graciously in it and I want to listen) or entitlement (I either do or don't deserve this). If I am in a tough marriage, I can live daily with a sense of entitlement and fail to perceive God's ways or I can seek to be thankful for what He is doing in it and listen to His voice of encouragement and wisdom. If I have been given great wealth, I can live with entitlement and believe that it is all about me or I can respond with thanksgiving and surrender to God's purposes. Entitlement hardens the heart, but gratitude softens the heart. With entitlement, God is a means to an end. With gratitude, God is the end, the goal, the prize.

Often, we are like kids on Christmas morning looking at the pair of pants our parents gave us. We might not hear the love spoken through the gift because we believe we are entitled to a new pair of pants, and therefore it is not seen as being a good gift.

When there is gratitude, we see life as a gift - even the hard things. When there is gratitude, we hear from God in all of life - even in the hard things. Gratitude opens our ears to hear the gentle voice of God.

Today, create a note that you can carry with you and keep in sight that says, "Give thanks in all circumstances; for this is the will of God in Christ Jesus for you." (1 Thessalonians 5:18-19) As you walk through your day, notice those times when entitlement rises up (e.g., "I don't deserve this." "Why me?" "I wish I had _____.") and pray this verse as you ask the Father to speak to you through the situation in question.

Pray this prayer as a simple statement of your desire:

Father, help me to silence every creature, including myself. I want to listen to You as I hear your voice. Help me to learn stillness so that I might be attentive to Your good and gracious voice. As I hear, may I have the courage to follow Your heart from my heart. Thank you for desiring to do life with me.

DECEMBER 10

He Softens Our Hearts As We Listen
Day 4

On that first Christmas Eve, an angel of the Lord appeared to a group of shepherds and said, "Fear not, for behold, I bring you good news of great joy that will be for all the people. For unto you is born this day in the city of David a Savior, who is Christ the Lord." (Luke 2:10-11)

It is fascinating that the first words were "fear not." The angel could have simply started with "Behold." Why "fear not?" First, the appearance of the angel was glorious and it frightened those humble shepherds. That makes sense. Second, hearing from God can be a little fearful. It is our deep desire, but what if He tells me to do something I don't want to do. Third, as humans, we tend to be fearful. "Do not fear" is the most common command in the Bible.

As we continue to ponder the challenge "if you hear His voice, don't harden your heart" (Hebrews 3 and Psalm 95), thinking through this issue of fear is significant. Quite simply, fear is the response we have to a perceived threat. Expression of fear can be either active or passive. We might express fear through passively cowering in the corner or we can express fear through actively fighting against things, taking life by the collar and not letting go. Ultimately, the threats we perceive have to do with our well-being. We ask questions like: "Is

41

life going to go ok for me?" "Am I going to be hurt?" "Am I going to make it?" "Will I ever get to _____?" "Will _____ ever stop?"

The challenge with fear is that it often runs in the background of our minds and hearts, subtly guiding and directing our responses and decisions. In his book, *Everything Belongs,* Richard Rohr writes:

> Our culture teaches us that everything out there is hostile. We have to compare, dominate, control, and insure. In brief, we have to be in charge. That need to be in charge moves us deeper and deeper into a world of anxiety.

As we are seeking to listen to God, fear is a challenge we need to address. It can keep us from hearing God and also listening to (trusting) God. So, how do we address the presence of fear in our lives?

First, we need to remember that God spoke to shepherds. In the first century, shepherds were not the heroes of the story like we often see in Christmas pageants. Shepherds were very common laborers who worked bad hours and were often away from their families. It was not a prestigious profession. They were everyday people! One of the fearful questions that can plague us is, "Will God speak to me? I'm nothing special." The simple answer is "Of course." Jesus describes Himself as a shepherd (John10:1-5). He came to us as one of us and His sheep can know His voice. It is not magic or superior knowledge that allows us to hear His voice. It is His goodness as a tender shepherd.

Second, we might be fearful that God will tell us to do something that we can't do or don't want to do. Here is the glorious truth: God always leads us in ways that connect with our deepest desires. We are hardwired to live in relationship with God. We may not always be aware of this truth and, in fact, may be more aware of other desires, but it is a truth which is deeper than all other truth. In Isaiah 55:1-2, God says to His people,

> Come, everyone who thirsts, come to the waters; and he who has no money, come, buy and eat! Come, buy wine and milk without money and without price. Why do you spend your money for that which is not bread, and your labor for that which does not satisfy? Listen diligently to me, and eat what is good, and delight yourselves in rich food.

The point is simply this: we tend to spend our resources (time, energy, and money) on things that can't satisfy our deepest longings, but if we "listen" to God, He graciously (freely) leads us to that which is good and ultimately satisfying. We can trust that. The first words from the Angel, after "don't be afraid," were "behold, I bring you good news of great joy that will be for all the people." The news that God brings is "joy." We can trust. Our deepest joy and God's heart are always in concert with one another.

Finally, we can approach a seemingly hostile world without fear as we learn to listen to God. His voice is one of calm and peace and rest. Fear is not from Him. Fear and anxiety are not part of His vocabulary. In Psalm 95, part of the foundation of listening to God is remembering that He is the creator: "Oh come, let us worship and bow down; let us kneel before the LORD, our Maker!" (v 6)

There are two significant ideas here. First, **we can let go of fear because He is the Creator.** This world is His and there is nothing beyond His knowledge or control. "In his hand are the depths of the earth; the heights of the mountains are his also. The sea is his, for he made it, and his hands formed the dry land." (v 4) The ancient peoples were afraid of the ocean. The mountains were the realm of bandits and thieves. God says, "no realm of life is outside My influence."

Second, **all of the created order contains the embedded message that we need not fear.** Anything that comes into our view can be an opportunity to listen to God. In Matthew 6, Jesus used flowers and birds to illustrate His challenge, "Do not be anxious." **Today**, as you walk through your day, ask God to speak to you through His creation. As you ponder the trees, the hills, the moon, the stars, the birds, or the flowers, … ask God to tell you about Himself. Hear His voice and listen (take it to heart and ponder it).

Utilize this prayer throughout your day as an expression of your trust:
Father, help me to silence every creature, including myself. I want to listen to You as I hear your voice. Help me to learn stillness so that I might be attentive to Your good and gracious voice. As I hear, may I have the courage to follow Your heart from my heart. Thank you for desiring to do life with me.

DECEMBER 11

He Softens Our Hearts As We Listen
Day 5

Part of learning to listen to God is becoming aware that we often hear and then listen to our false-self. Our false sense of self speaks within our heart and says, "You need to have (certain things) to be significant" or "You need to do (certain things) to be respected" or "You need people to treat you (a certain way) in order to feel worthy."

Our false-self operates independently of God and demands that its desires be fulfilled. When they aren't, we feel a sense of unworthiness. We might have this nagging sense that things aren't right – that something is wrong with us. This leads to sin - a striving to make our false-self feel better without God. Then, people in our lives become those who either affirm or deny our false-self. People are no longer recipients of our love, but objects that we desire or despise. The challenge of this self-talk is that it's frequently happening below the surface of our conscious awareness.

In the Christmas songs "O Holy Night," we find the line, "Long lay the world in sin and error pining, **til He appeared and the soul felt its worth**." This lyric beautifully illustrates what happens when we live from our false-self. The "pining" describes the desires of the false-self which always leads to sin and error (i.e., living independently of God and struggling to live in relationship with others). When we live according to the voice of the false-self, there is not room for God or others in our hearts.

The answer to the problem of the false-self is beautifully described in the second half of this lyric. When Jesus appeared, the soul felt its **worth**. Rather than listening to the voice of the false-self, Jesus speaks a new truth into our souls. How does this work? How is it that the soul feels its worth? Consider the Apostle Paul's words:

> For the grace of God has appeared, bringing salvation for all people, training us to renounce ungodliness and worldly passions, and to live self-controlled, upright, and godly lives in the present age, waiting for our blessed hope, the appearing of the glory of our great God and Savior Jesus Christ, who gave himself for us to redeem us from all lawlessness and to purify for himself a people for his own possession who are zealous for good works.
> Titus 2:11-14

Notice all the richness of this passage: when His grace (Jesus) appears, we are brought into a relationship with God ("bringing salvation") as we trust in Him. Then, we are (by His grace) taught to renounce "worldly passions" which are the voices (the demands) of the false-self.

His grace is the beautiful message: we are loved without condition, we are strong when we are weak, and we are significant because we belong to Him. His grace teaches us that we don't need anything that

the false-self desires and demands. Also, notice the word "wait" …
even when we feel "less than" or unworthy, we can wait because
there is more of the story to be revealed. Finally, we belong to Him
("a people for his own possession") which ensures that we are secure
and strong and significant.

Are you listening to the demeaning voice of the false-self that
says you are lacking and therefore need to strive to prove your
worth? Or, **are you listening to God who speaks grace** over your
life again and again which allows you to stop and rest?

Make no mistake! When you hear, "I don't belong" or "I'm not good
enough" or "There is something wrong with me", this is not the
voice of God. God speaks love and grace and acceptance because, in
Christ, this is what is most true about us. We are recipients of His
love, grace and acceptance. When we keep listening to the voice of
the false-self, we will be led back into sin (living independently of
God) over and over again.

It gets tricky when we consider that sin and weakness will be a part of
our lives. However, we can learn to renounce or "say no" to the
demands of the false-self as a response to our sin and weakness when
we listen to His grace. Writer, Simone Weil, illustrates how our
listening can change:

> Two prisoners whose cells adjoin communicate with each
> other by knocking on the wall. The wall is the thing which
> separates them but is also their means of communication. It is
> the same with us and God. Every separation is a link.

Here's the point: let your sin, your weakness, be the **connecting point with God rather than a dividing line**. When you are feeling that sense of disconnected, unworthiness, or lack, let that be your cue to listen to God, to let Him in.

Today, practice listening to His voice as it relates to your sin and weakness. When you are confronted with the voice of the false-self, stop and ask God what He wants to say. If words other than grace arise, calmly say "no" to them. Wait and listen for the soft, gentle but strong voice of God who "will rejoice over you with gladness; he will quiet you by his love" (Zephaniah 3:17). As you hear His voice, don't harden your heart but listen and, therefore, act out of that foundation of love rather than the false-self.

Take a few minutes and practice this now.

Begin with this prayer and then sit quietly before Him:

Father, help me to silence every creature, including myself. I want to listen to You as I hear your voice. Help me to learn stillness so that I might be attentive to Your good and gracious voice. As I hear, may I have the courage to follow Your heart from my heart. Thank you for desiring to do life with me.

He Softens Our Hearts as We Listen
Day 6

Jesus was born into a world of pain and suffering. From the time of His birth, He lived the paradox of being absolutely safe in the plan of eternity but also experiencing suffering. As a young boy, his family moved to a foreign country in order to evade a murderous king. The king went ahead and gave it his best shot:

> Then Herod, when he saw that he had been tricked by the wise men, became furious, and he sent and killed all the male children in Bethlehem and in all that region who were two years old or under, according to the time that he had ascertained from the wise men. (Matthew 2:16)

This was a horrible, senseless slaughter. We are wise not to miss the reality that pain and suffering is not ignored in the Gospel. God is not afraid to talk about it. He is sensitive to suffering and does not run away from its presence in the world. On the one hand, the great hope of the Gospel is that one day: "He will wipe away every tear from their eyes, and death shall be no more, neither shall there be mourning, nor crying, nor pain anymore, for the former things have passed away." (Revelation 21:4) On the other hand, until that future day, God speaks to us and uses our pain and suffering.

In *The Problem of Pain*, C. S. Lewis suggests:

We can ignore even pleasure. But pain insists upon being attended to. God whispers to us in our pleasures, speaks in our conscience, but shouts in our pains: it is his megaphone to rouse a deaf world.

Suffering, if we engage with it, opens our ears to hear God in ways we don't when life is merrily humming along. It's not that God actually shouts in our pains, it's that we have the opportunity to be more sensitive and open.

If you are experiencing some kind of suffering in your life, you have choices. You can **distance** yourself from it through running away to new relationships, new circumstances, new *whatever*. You can **deny** that the suffering is even going on through acting like nothing is really wrong … this can be a flat denial or a "religious sugar coating" which ignores the hurt and pain of suffering through platitude. You can also **despair** though hanging your head and letting the pain be the only reality in your life. But there is another way … the way of **dependence**. It is a place of listening and attending to God. Most often, we can't know the why of suffering but we can experience God's voice in deep, significant ways. Oswald Chambers counsels:

> Are you in the dark right now in your circumstances, or in your life with God? If so, then remain quiet. If you open your mouth in the dark, you will speak while in the wrong mood— darkness is the time to listen. Don't talk to other people about it; don't read books to find out the reason for the darkness; just listen and obey. If you talk to other people, you cannot hear what God is saying.

Suffering and pain brings the gift of a softened heart … if we let it …

if we listen. The Apostle Paul dealt with a thorn, a suffering, that would not go away. He prayed and listened. And, he prayed and listened. God spoke to Him clearly, "My grace is sufficient for you, for my power is made perfect in weakness." (2 Cor. 12:9) Suffering can be a gift because it can strip us of our independence and self-sufficiency. If living a life of dependence upon God is not a value, then pain will never have a purpose in our lives. Certainly, there are large picture ways that God uses suffering and some of that will not be apparent until eternity, but for now, He graciously uses pain to shape and mold us. Will we let Him? Will we listen to the message He has for us in our suffering?

Today, consider the following: what suffering is present in your life? How have you been thinking about and speaking about your pain? Stop and ask God, *What is your message for me in all of this?* You may not hear for a while, so be persistent. It can take time for all the other voices to quiet. When you do hear, be ready to listen!

Once again, pray these words from your heart:

> *Father, help me to silence every creature, including myself. I want to listen to You as I hear your voice. Help me to learn stillness so that I might be attentive to Your good and gracious voice. As I hear, may I have the courage to follow Your heart from my heart. Thank you for desiring to do life with me.*

DECEMBER 13

He Softens Our Hearts as We Listen Day 7

In Matthew 1:18-25, we learn that an angel appeared to Joseph, the earthly father of Jesus, and addressed him as "Joseph, Son of David." It's interesting that the tag "Son of David" is used. If an angel is speaking to you, it would seem that "hey you" would suffice in grabbing one's attention, but there is something significant going on. "Son of David" was part of Joseph's identity. It placed him in the line of Messiah (the promised Savior) who would be a descendant of David. The angel was reminding Joseph about his identity. In the very next verses, we see the interplay between name and identity again:

> All this took place to fulfill what the Lord had spoken by the prophet: 'Behold, the virgin shall conceive and bear a son, and they shall call his name Immanuel' (which means, God with us). When Joseph woke from sleep, he did as the angel of the Lord commanded him: he took his wife, but knew her not until she had given birth to a son. And he called his name Jesus.

Again, name is significant. For the baby who was born, two names are highlighted in three short verses: Immanuel (God with us) and Jesus (Hebrew: Yeshua for Yahweh saves). Name is identity. In our modern world, we've lost a full sense of identity. We frequently think of ourselves based on what we do or what we look like or what others think of us. However, God speaks to us based on our name (our true identity) and we listen and pray based on His name (His true identity).

People often ask, "How do I know if God is speaking to me?" Discernment is certainly needed. It is important that we know the name (identity) of the One we are seeking and that we are letting Him speak to the real us … the depths of us which are not completely known even to us.

In John 10:3-5, we are introduced to an image of Jesus as shepherd and Jesus says this:

> To him the gatekeeper opens. The sheep hear his voice, and he calls his own sheep by name and leads them out. When he has brought out all his own, he goes before them, and the sheep follow him, for they know his voice. A stranger they will not follow, but they will flee from him, for they do not know the voice of strangers.

Three ideas stand out in these verses: *we hear his voice; he calls us by name;* and *we know His voice.* These are deep, significant realities. First, **God does speak and we can hear!** It is not the special or elite, but the child of God, redeemed by the blood of the lamb, who can hear. It is part of who we are. Second, **He speaks to us based on our identity.** He doesn't speak to us and lead us based on *who we'd like to be* or *who others think we are* or *even our failures and sin.* He knows our true identity as forgiven, renewed, made-in-the-image-of-God people. He knows this better than we do. He knows the unique ways He made us and the unique plans He has for us. How often do we approach God based on identities that are not our core? How often do we come to God and seek Him based on what we do rather than who we are? Finally, **we trustingly follow because we know His name**.

Several questions flow from these realities:

1. Am I regularly putting myself into a place to listen? It is a high privilege and also a necessity for being led by the God of the universe.

2. Am I listening based on my perceived identity or allowing Him to speak to places in me that I may not even fully know? We are led into abundant life (the following verses in John 10) as we listen to our true name.

3. How well do I know His identity? What are the kinds of things that He says?

This concept of "name" is the reason that we are encouraged to pray things in the "name of Jesus" (John 14:13). It is not the name, per se, that is significant but the identity that is represented in the name. So, we pray "in the name of Jesus" not as a magic tagline at the end of a prayer, but as a reminder that we are praying based on His character and trusting His character. When we pray in Jesus' name, we are submitting ourselves to His identity, His goodness and sovereignty and grace. Silent, restful prayer is frequently the best way to pray in Jesus' name, trusting in Him. Mother Theresa of Calcutta commented,

We need to find God, and He cannot be found in noise and restlessness. God is the friend of silence. See how nature — trees, flowers, grass — grows in silence; see the stars, the moon and sun, how they move in silence. ... The more we receive in silent prayer, the more we can give in our active life. We need silence to be able to touch souls. The essential thing is not what we say, but what God says to us and through us. All our words will be useless unless they come from within — words which do not give the light of Christ increase the darkness.

If listening to God is new (and even if it's not), **ask the Father what He wants to call you**! Our listening needs to be on His terms if we want to live into all that He has planned for us.

Today, set aside a few minutes and simply sit quietly before God. As other thoughts or emotions come into your perception, let them go … entrusting them to the Father. Then, read the words from John 10:1-4. Next, ask the Father, "What do want to call me?" Sit quietly and listen. Remember, He may just want to sit quietly with you. He may just want you to rest in His presence. Asking the question alone is an act of trust and surrender and, today, that may be just what He desires.

As we prepare Him room in our hearts, we began with learning to wait and then this next element of learning to listen. As we wait, He humbles our hearts. As we listen, He softens our hearts because we are learning to trust His name and our name.

Put this prayer into your own words ...

Father, help me to silence every creature, including myself. I want to listen to You as I hear your voice. Help me to learn stillness so that I might be attentive to Your good and gracious voice. As I hear, may I have the courage to follow Your heart from my heart. Thank you for desiring to do life with me.

DECEMBER 14

He Expands Our Hearts as We Release Day 1

Advent ... a time of waiting and longing and desire. We live into this season of the church calendar in order to fully experience our deepest desires for Messiah. We were created to live moment by moment in the satisfaction of relationship with Him. So, as we pay attention to that desire, it makes possible the experience of that desire.

Frequently, we live at the surface of desire, toying around with things and people and activities, unaware that infinite joy is ours. This joy is found in the depths of our being. We **learn to wait** so that we *discover* Him anew. **We learn to listen** so that we begin to *trust* Him. Now, we **learn to release** all other desires so that we experience *inner healing*.

We all have the tendency to put up protective walls around our hearts. When we experience hurt or disappointment, there is a natural instinct to say "never again" and we put up a protective wall. This hardens our hearts ... it shrinks our hearts so that we don't put ourselves "out there" to be hurt all over again. Consequently, there is not room to live and move and breathe freely. We live at the surface of desire because our hearts are small and crowded with all the protective artillery of an army ready to defend at a moment's notice. At one level or another, this is the human experience. This explains why we struggle to live at peace with others. It explains why we get hurt so easily or lash out so frequently. Thankfully, God doesn't leave us there. In Christ, we are brought into God's family with the opportunity to experience renovated hearts.

How does this work? In Psalm 119:32, the writer declares, "I will run in the way of your commandments when you enlarge my heart!" An enlarged heart is one which is free to run after God with abandon. This is the work of God in our lives as we learn to release and let go of all but Him. In John 10, we learn more as Jesus speaks of being our shepherd and leading us as we listen to His voice. Where does He lead us? Jesus adds to the shepherd image as He says,

> I am the door. If anyone enters by me, he will be saved and will go in and out and find pasture. The thief comes only to steal and kill and destroy. **I came that they may have life and have it abundantly.** I am the good shepherd. The good shepherd lays down his life for the sheep. (v. 9-11)

The picture of salvation here is bigger than simply being saved from hell (although it includes that). It is an image of being able to move in and out of the sheep pen … finding our sustenance in "abundance." Jesus says that this abundance of life is possible. It is also possible that we listen to the voice of the thief. What is that voice? It is the voice that says, "You're on your own. You better protect yourself because no one else will." It is the voice that says, "You can't really live a life with God. That is for others, not you." It is the voice that says, "You should just do whatever you want, because this life with God can't be trusted. God is just trying to control you." Jesus says it is the voice of a thief because he wants to steal and kill any hope that is present. These voices of the thief are the very reason why we have protective walls in our hearts. These voices of the thief explain why our hearts are often so small.

As we begin to listen to His voice, we will hear Him say, "Come back … return … let go … release." In Isaiah 30:15-16, God graciously calls His people to a place of renewal. Notice the words that are used.

> For thus said the Lord GOD, the Holy One of Israel, "In returning and rest you shall be saved; in quietness and in trust shall be your strength." But you were unwilling, and you said, "No! We will flee upon horses"; therefore you shall flee away; and, "We will ride upon swift steeds."

The word "saved" speaks of being delivered and rescued by God in this life. We experience that as we return to Him. The word "return" could also be translated as repentance.

Repentance is one of those words which has been turned into a harsh word screamed by preachers. However, repent is one of the most beautiful words known to man. It makes sense that the "thief" would distort the word in our thinking, because "repent" is a word which speaks of return and renewal and rejoicing. We repent when we let go of finding our strength in anything but Him.

Notice that the people of Israel were unwilling because they wanted to put their trust in horses. To our modern ears, it sounds quaint and strange but horses were the ancient symbol of power and strength and wealth. If one had a horse, he or she could travel or flee danger or pursue dreams. God offered Himself but the people wanted horses. We are often in the same place. God offers Himself but we want (you can fill in the blank).

Finally, God also says that it is in "quietness and trust" that we are strengthened. God graciously calls us to let go, to release all else but Him. The problem is that we can feel very weak. In quiet, we listen and learn to trust because letting go can feel like death! That's because letting go involves a kind of dying. The great writer and woman of God, Elisabeth Elliot said, "Many deaths must go into reaching our maturity in Christ, many letting goes."

Brother Lawrence commented that,

> The heart must be emptied of all other things, because God will possess the heart alone; and as He cannot possess it alone without emptying it of all besides, so neither can He act there, and do in it what He pleases, unless it be left vacant to Him.

As we walk this mortal coil, we often feel that paradox of desiring God and yet desiring other things. The beauty of learning to release and let go is that God graciously invites us to let go. He doesn't force us. He desires for us to come with open hands so that He can fill them. And, this is a process that goes on day by day as He invites us anew. It's a relationship that has to be nurtured. He doesn't overwhelm, but leads us one step at a time. The paradox will be there and it's ok because He is never all we want until He is all we have. Jesus alone is the hope of the Gospel and He leads us to open fields of abundance.

What do you need to release today? Don't worry about all that you need to release but what is it today? Quiet yourself before Him and simply ask, "Father, what shall I release today?"

Father, I admit that I am a bundle of paradoxes. I want to live in You alone. I confess this is my deepest desire and yet I have other desires. Today, give me the courage to let go. Give me the strength to repent. Give me eyes to see those places of strength to which I cling that I might release all to You. Thank you for Your patience and grace and leading in my life. Enlarge my heart. Amen.

DECEMBER 15

He Expands Our Hearts as We Release Day 2

Expectations have a way of shaping our perception of reality. And, most of the time we are unaware of our expectations. We wear expectations like a pair of glasses that filter out what we don't want and lock in on what we do.

Most people missed the entrance of Jesus into the world because He came in a very unexpected way. He was born in a feeding trough for animals in a cave behind an inn for travelers. It was very uneventful. In the same way, Jesus' entrance into Jerusalem as an adult was equally unexpected.

> Rejoice greatly, O daughter of Zion! Shout aloud, O daughter
> of Jerusalem! Behold, your king is coming to you; righteous
> and having salvation is he, humble and mounted on a
> donkey, on a colt, the foal of a donkey. (Zechariah 9:9;
> Matthew 21:5)

Most would have expected the King to come on a horse (a symbol of victory and power). Additionally, the birth of a King, one would think, would be in a royal family with pomp and circumstance. There were actually rumors throughout Jesus' life that he was born illegitimately.

Today, we can miss the work and presence of God in our lives because we expect. We expect that God would work in this way or that way. It might be that we don't expect suffering. In fact, we expect "blessing" that looks like ease and pleasure and good times. Then, when suffering is present, we have no way of seeing God at work.

Or, it could be that we expect people to treat us a certain way and when they don't, we can't imagine that God could be in it. The list could go on, but expectations have a way of blurring our vision.

Further, expectations can shift our hearts to a dark place. Gerald May made the observation that "Expectations are premeditated resentments." Our hearts don't see what they want to see and consequently move into a place of bitterness.

Do you find yourself bitter or resentful about anything in your life? Notice the counsel of 1 Peter 5:6-7, "Humble yourselves, therefore, under the mighty hand of God so that at the proper time he may exalt you, casting all your anxieties on him, because he cares for you."

How do we humble ourselves? By trusting God with our anxieties. The issue is not the bitterness (the need to humble oneself) per se, but the anxiety underneath it. Anxiety is the internal struggle created when expectations don't match experience.

Releasing expectations is essential if we are going to move into all that God desires for us. Anxiety has a way of shrinking our hearts so that there is not room for God. Physically, we may even feel muscle tension or shortness of breath. As we release expectations, our hearts expand and are able to hold whatever is and however God is involved.

Meister Eckhart observed, "God is not attained by a process of addition to anything in the soul, but by a process of subtraction." As we subtract expectations, we suddenly have room for God. We don't do this by trying to control our anxiety and expectations but by "releasing" them ("casting all your anxieties"). We can do this because He cares about us. We can let go because He has plans and ways that are loving and gracious and wise and perfect.

Expectations are best discerned by looking at our anxieties. Spend a few minutes prayerfully asking, "What am I anxious about?" Then, consider: what are the expectations underneath that anxiety? Once you've identified the expectation, release it as you simply pray: *Father, I know you care so I let go of my grip on this version of reality.* Meditate on 1 Peter 5:6-7 and repeat this exercise as you are able throughout the day.

> *Father, I admit that I am a bundle of paradoxes. I want to live in You alone. I confess this is my deepest desire and yet I have other desires. Today, give me the courage to let go. Give me the strength to repent. Give me eyes to see those places of strength to which I cling that I might release all to You. Thank you for Your patience and grace and leading in my life. Enlarge my heart. Amen.*

He Expands Our Hearts as We Release Day 3

The Christmas story is one of joy and peace and hope. We see those words sprinkled around in the decorations of the seasons, but they describe the end of the story instead of the beginning. To get to the end, we always have to start at the beginning. The key word that describes the beginning is incarnation, which speaks of Jesus coming "in the flesh." This is clear from John 1:14, "The Word became flesh and dwelt among us."

But, why is this significant? Because it means that Jesus came to get His hands dirty ... to live in the mess of this world. By living in the midst of it, He was able to bring joy and peace and hope. And what does this mean for us? Along with incarnation, the other words that would be more helpful would be invasion and infiltration. He came to invade our lives and go behind enemy lines. It's hard to see such an intensity in the small hands and tiny feet of a baby, but it's all there if you look hard enough.

The question each of us has to ask ourselves is, will I let Him in ... past my lines of defense? As we learn to listen to Him, we begin to trust as our hearts are softened. Then, the next step of trust is to release. Will I release myself to Him? Will I let Him have His way?

It can get tricky because He is not a demanding, severe God. We can mistake His gentleness for nonchalance as we say, "It's not that big of a deal if I hold on to this one part of my life." Is He gracious and patient? Yes! But, it is a big deal. As we release and let go, we find life … His life unfolding inside of us. Do you have a vision for what this life might be like?

The great C. S. Lewis suggested the following:

> Imagine yourself as a living house. God comes in to rebuild that house. At first, perhaps, you can understand what He is doing. He is getting the drains right and stopping the leaks in the roof and so on; you knew that those jobs needed doing and so you are not surprised. But presently He starts knocking the house about in a way that hurts abominably and does not seem to make any sense. What on earth is He up to? The explanation is that He is building quite a different house from the one you thought of – throwing out a new wing here, putting on an extra floor there, running up towers, making courtyards. You thought you were being made into a decent little cottage: but He is building a palace. He intends to come and live in it Himself.

Is there a part of your life to which you are clinging? Is there something that you are not releasing? Are you holding up the remodeling project? Often, we are resistant to God's plans but we aren't even fully aware. How do we know if there are parts of our lives in which we are resistant? There are three primary ways we resist:

1. We can act like everything in our lives is okay. (denial)

2. We can compare ourselves to others and proclaim that we're not that bad.

3. We can talk about theological truth but keep it abstract.

The gracious remodeling project is ongoing in this life. Jesus desires to keep expanding and growing the capacity of hearts so that we might experience more and more of Him. The Apostle Paul talks about us being "filled with all the fullness of God." (Ephesians 3:19) That is the hope! That is the vision.

What do you need to release? What wall do you need to let Him knock down? Start with resistance. Pray and ask God to show you places where you are resistant. As you see it, release specific control as you pray, "My body is a temple of the Holy Spirit. I am not my own because I was bought with a price." (1 Corinthians 6:19-20)

Today, as you walk through your day, pray this prayer as the Spirit brings it to your mind:

> *Father, I admit that I am a bundle of paradoxes. I want to live in You alone. I confess this is my deepest desire and yet I have other desires. Today, give me the courage to let go. Give me the strength to repent. Give me eyes to see those places of strength to which I cling that I might release all to You. Thank you for Your patience and grace and leading in my life. Enlarge my heart. Amen.*

He Expands Our Hearts as We Release Day 4

As we continue to walk toward Christmas in this season of Advent, we are wise to consider how Mary prepared room in her heart for the Messiah. Mary was challenged to make room in her body to carry the Christ child, but it started with her heart. Mary was not an unwilling participant but she asked questions and pondered what it would mean to welcome the divine into her life in such a personal way.

We are invited to make room in our hearts for Christ as well so that we might display Him for the world to see.

Mary was approached by an angel and immediately she began to consider the nature of what was going on. The angel called her "favored one" and Luke 1:29 says that "she was greatly troubled at the saying, and tried to discern what sort of greeting this might be." The idea of "troubled" meant that she was not taking this lightly and understood that something significant was happening. Next, the angel shared that she will become pregnant and bear the Messiah. Rather than jump for joy at being chosen, she began to realize the cost and asked questions. She realized that this would mean her world would be thrown upside down.

How often do we fail to count the costs? We jump right in with joy at the prospect of God being at work in our lives and don't ask the appropriate questions. Certainly, there is joy but we have to consider and ponder what it will mean to make room in our lives for Messiah. Mary asks the simple question, "How will this be, since I am a virgin?" (Luke 1:34) More than a simple logistical question, I wonder if Mary was also considering, "What will this do to my reputation? Am I going to have to let go of my hope to get married and have a family?" Mary had to let go of her identity as a good young girl who was preparing to be married. We know from later accounts in the Gospels (cf. Mark 6:3, John 8:41) that people questioned the legitimacy of Jesus' birth as they hinted at him being born out of wedlock.

Part of making room in our hearts for Christ is releasing our identity. We may see ourselves for what we are: teachers, doctors, builders, mothers, fathers, nurses, writers, caregivers, waiters, sons, daughters, spouses, etc. We might also see ourselves for what we are not: married (or, happily married), parents, gainfully employed, well-off, appreciated, etc. The list can fluctuate from season to season but whenever our identity is in anything but Christ first, we will struggle in making room for Him in our lives. As human beings, we were not designed to hold on to any of these other identities for our sense of worth or strength or love. Christ will always get crowded out or reduced to simply helping us find our worth in these other identities. We are invited to let go – to release – these other places where we might find our identity.

Mary received that invitation and said, "Behold, I am the servant of the Lord; let it be to me according to your word." (Luke 1:38)

We were created to live with a sense of identity in Him … relying upon Him to be our deepest sense of worth and strength and love. When we choose to see ourselves primarily in light of some other identity, we are running from our created design. During the Christmas season, we can struggle particularly with not feeling love or worth (perhaps even descending into the pit of loneliness) as we look at everyone else's "perfect" Christmas cards.

Henri Nouwen, in speaking about identity, offered this:

> Your true identity is as a child of God. This is the identity you have to accept. Once you have claimed it and settled in it, you can live in a world that gives you much joy as well as pain. You can receive the praise as well as the blame that comes to you as an opportunity for strengthening your basic identity, because the identity that makes you free is anchored beyond all human praise and blame. You belong to God.

He goes on to say that we often allow others to become a part of our basic identity and we feel that we cannot live without them.

> But they could not fulfill that divine role, so they left you, and you felt abandoned. But it is precisely that experience of abandonment that called you back to your true identity as a child of God. Only God can fully dwell in that deepest place in you and give you a sense of safety. But the danger remains that you will let other people run away with your sacred center, thus throwing you into anguish.

To prepare that room in our hearts, there are identities that we must release. Today, as you walk through your day, ask the Father to make you aware of those places and times when you are resting in some identity other than as a child of God. Emotions can often be our clearest clue that our identity is in something other than Jesus. It begins with trusting that you were made for something deeper than being in a certain relationship or having certain things or doing certain things. As you are aware of identifying with anything other than Christ, simply stop and proclaim, "I am a child of God, safe and secure and loved in Him." This allows the releasing to begin and, as you release, He is able to inhabit your heart in ever deepening ways.

Begin now, take a few minutes and ask the Father to show you those "other identities" that you may be holding. Then take a few minutes and put the following prayer into your own words:

Father, I admit that I am a bundle of paradoxes. I want to live in You alone. I confess this is my deepest desire and yet I have other desires. Today, give me the courage to let go. Give me the strength to repent. Give me eyes to see those places of strength to which I cling that I might release all to You. Thank you for Your patience and grace and leading in my life. Enlarge my heart. Amen.

He Expands Our Hearts as We Release Day 5

"They shall call his name Immanuel which means, God with us."
(Matthew 1:23)

Jesus was born so that the truth of "God with us" could be reality in each of our lives. The very essence of life is "God with us." We were created to be with God. Our lives are full and meaningful when we are with God … doing life with Him. It is an intensely relational reality and we are relational beings!

Sin is doing life without God. It is exactly what Adam and Eve did in the beginning. They decided to go it alone and that "stance" led to the act of doing what God had told them not to do – eat the fruit. We engage in sinful acts when we decide to go it alone.

We can stay in this "stance" and act out of it. However, Christmas and the coming of Jesus into the world means that we can do life from a "God with us" stance – depending upon Him. If we have entered into a relationship with God through trusting Jesus Christ as Messiah, "God with us" is the fundamental truth of our lives. However, we may not be living in that truth … it may not be our fundamental experience. Living in that reality (which is the deepest desire of our lives) requires releasing.

When we are living independently, our hearts are small. We have those protective walls up because what is most real is our pain, our separation from God, our loneliness. So, we act on what we believe is in our best interests. When we move into the reality of "God with us," our hearts expand and we are able to act out of love for God and others. Again, it requires a releasing. We have to let go in order to experience what is most true about us in Christ.

The writer of Hebrews challenges us, "If you hear his voice, don't harden you hearts." This speaks to listening, but he also talks about the releasing that happens after we listen to the call of God. When we are captured by the vision of the "God with us" life, we are listening and our hearts soften. Next, comes the releasing:

> But exhort one another every day, as long as it is called 'today,' that none of you may be hardened by the deceitfulness of sin. (3:13)

What is the deceitfulness of sin? Think of it this way: if sin is the stance of living independently of God, then the deceitfulness of sin refers to **beliefs we hold about the benefits of doing life independently of God**.

The reality is that we are only truly happy when we are doing life with God. So, we are encouraged to let go of the erroneous beliefs that tell us, "you will be happy if _____." True joy is not dependent upon doing something, being something, or having a specific circumstance in our lives. It is our reality that we experience when we let go of all else but this gracious gift of God with us.

What beliefs about your happiness do you need to release? Here's a list of potential "deceitfulness of sin" statements:

> I will be happy if I do good things.
> I will be happy if I feel loved.
> I will be happy if I feel admired.
> I will be happy if I feel unique.
> I will be happy if I can be competent.
> I will be happy if I can have security.
> I will be happy if I can be content.
> I will be happy if I am in control.
> I will be happy if I am at peace.

Ignatius of Loyola spoke to this challenge to release when he said,
> It is necessary that we become indifferent to all created things so that, on our part, we want not health rather than sickness, riches rather than poverty, honor rather than dishonor, long rather than short life, and so in all the rest; desiring and choosing only what helps us praise, reverence, and serve God.

How do we become "indifferent to all created things" and therefore open to the true joy of an expanded heart that can hold the love of God and others? We release. How do we know what to release? Pay attention to your emotions because they are reliable indicators of what you believe will make you happy. As you notice agitation, restlessness, unhappiness, loneliness, or anger, ask yourself what you are believing will make you happy.

Begin with the list above and prayerfully ask God for insight into your life. It may come quickly or you may have to stay with it for a while. What are your "deceitfulness of sin" statements? Next, ask the Lord to make you aware of your emotions throughout the day. When you notice something, stop, release, and pray this Psalm:

> Nevertheless, I am continually with you; you hold my right hand. You guide me with your counsel, and afterward you will receive me to glory. Whom have I in heaven but you? And there is nothing on earth that I desire besides you. My flesh and my heart may fail, but God is the strength of my heart and my portion forever. (Psalm 73:23-26)

Releasing begins with a fundamental belief that life is only found in a "God with us" life and an understanding that we are in need of that life. We need to release and let go of old ways of thinking.

Father, I admit that I am a bundle of paradoxes. I want to live in You alone. I confess this is my deepest desire and yet I have other desires. Today, give me the courage to let go. Give me the strength to repent. Give me eyes to see those places of strength to which I cling that I might release all to You. Thank you for Your patience and grace and leading in my life. Enlarge my heart. Amen.

He Expands Our Hearts as We Release Day 6

When Jesus, the Messiah, entered into human history, He did so in an incredibly quiet and vulnerable manner. Indeed, could it have been any quieter? He was born into a poor, common family in an out of the way place. He wasn't born in the most important city of his country. He wasn't born in the most important country in his region. He was born in a country that was under foreign occupation.

Why were things so quiet? Why didn't He come with fanfare and publicity and Messiah written across the sky in flashing lights? All would have been possible but not consistent with God's character. He never forces Himself on us. He will not demand ....

The Scriptures tell us that wise men (magi) came to the Christ child (Matthew 2:1-12). They were not, however, on the scene the night Jesus was born. They showed up at some point in the first two years. The wise men saw a star from their homes in the East (likely Persia) and discerned that it was a king. Notice that Jesus' birth and its significance was lost on those who were much closer, those who knew the prophecies of Scripture. These wise men noticed ... they saw what others did not. And then, they listened to what they saw and came to worship. We don't know a lot more about the wise men, but *The Magnificent Defeat,* by Frederick Buechner, imagines what might have happened to the wise men (as told by one of them):

> But why did we go? I could not tell you now, and I could not have told you then, not even as we were in the very process of going. Not that we had no motive but that we had so many. Curiosity, I suppose: to be wise is to be eternally curious, and we were very wise. We want to see for ourselves this One before whom even the stars are said to bow down – to see perhaps if it was really true because even the wise have their doubts. And longing. Longing. Why will a man who is dying of thirst crawl miles across sands as hot as fire at simply the possibility of water? Why will a man labor and struggle all the days of his life so that in the end he has something to give the one he loves?

> I will tell you two terrible things. What we saw on the face of the new-born child was his death. A fool could have seen it as well. It sat on his head like a crown or a bat, this death he would die. And we saw, as sure as the earth beneath our feet, that to stay with him would be to share that death, and that is why we left – giving only our gifts, withholding the rest.

> And now, brothers, I will ask you a terrible question, and God knows I ask it also to myself. Is the truth beyond all truths, beyond the stars, just this: that to live without him is the real death, that to die with him is the only life?

Indeed, it makes sense that the wise men saw the jealousy of King Herod and his murderous plans to kill any children within the age range of Jesus, and thought, "We're out of here." What they didn't understand is that we find true life when we let go of our perceived sense of life. How often do we come with our gifts but leave with our life, as we know it, intact? Jesus said, "For whoever would save his life will lose it, but whoever loses his life for my sake will save it." (Luke 9:24)

The word "save" speaks of protecting and holding on and "losing" speaks of letting go. The irony of "protecting" what we perceive to be "life" is that we will miss out on what is "truly life." We have a tendency to hold on to all kinds of things (things that we think we control) to give us life. The paradox of Jesus' statement in Luke is that we are actually imprisoned by that which we cling to for life … it slowly kills us. He alone gives life in the freedom of relationship with Him. It is a life that is free because He does all the "holding" and we are free to use our hands to love Him and others. We are free to enjoy what is, not live imprisoned by what is not. We are free from needing anything because in Christ, we have everything.

Ignatius of Loyola wisely offers:

> Detachment comes only if we have a stronger attachment; therefore our one dominating desire and fundamental choice must be to live in the loving presence and wisdom of Christ, our Savior.

Jesus won't pry our hands off of our life. He invites us to let go (to detach), which will happen as we have a vision for what is better. We struggle because we have mixed emotions about what we cling to for life. We have mixed emotions about what Jesus says is life (Him alone). Alan Jones shares:

> The task of love is … to lay us bare, to set us free. But we love the prison-house. The plan of bondage is, at least, familiar. Love, then, comes as an unwelcome shock. The very thing we think we want, we dread.

Jesus models this way of "detached" living in Philippians 2. "…though he was in the form of God, did not count equality with God a thing to be grasped, but made himself nothing, taking the form of a servant, being born in the likeness of men." Two observations and two questions flow from this text.

1. His "equality with God" was not something He "grasped" or literally, "used for his own advantage. Jesus' most significant personal reality (His deity) was not something that He used for Himself.

   How do you view the "strengths" of your life (and we all have them)?

2. He "made himself nothing" or literally, "he poured himself out." Jesus let go of his life so that he could love.

   What do you need to let go of?

Sit with those questions and ask a good, gracious Father who only wants to give life.

> *Father, I admit that I am a bundle of paradoxes. I want to live in You alone. I confess this is my deepest desire and yet I have other desires. Today, give me the courage to let go. Give me the strength to repent. Give me eyes to see those places of strength to which I cling that I might release all to You. Thank you for Your patience and grace and leading in my life. Enlarge my heart. Amen.*

DECEMBER 20

He Expands Our Hearts as We Release
Day 7

It's tragic that we can be so filled with knowledge and yet not know God. After Jesus was born, the wise men arrived in Jerusalem and asked about the coming king, the Messiah. The religious people in Jerusalem knew the answer. They knew the Bible verses. What they had missed is that Jesus had been born only six miles away in Bethlehem. Jesus had been born right under their noses and they missed it.

They were so busy that they missed God's interjection of Himself into the world. We can get so busy that we miss all those moments every day when God is interjecting Himself into our world. Those who stop to notice, see Him everywhere and experience Him in all things. Paul affirms this in Romans 8. "God works in all things for the good."

It can be so difficult to see! Our hearts can be so full of "other things" and our perception clouded by our knowledge. In one sense, knowledge can actually blind us. The logic is this: if we know, then we can get busy doing what we see and choosing what we believe is right. However, God is right in front of us and all around us … desiring to be "with us" … and we miss Him. Anthony de Mello builds on this theme:

85

The fact is that you are surrounded by God and yet you don't see God, because you 'know' about Him. The final barrier to the vision of God is our God concept. You miss God because you think you know. That's the terrible thing about religion. That's what the Gospels were saying – that religious people 'knew,' so they got rid of Jesus. The highest knowledge of God is to know God as unknowable.

Knowing God as unknowable puts us in a place of humility in which we slow down enough in our hearts, minds, and body to perceive Him. The paradox is striking. When we think we know, we miss Him. When we acknowledge that we do not know, we begin to see. Our knowledge has a place but it must submit to our actual experience of and seeking of God in all things.

So, how do we live in this place of knowing that we don't know? Let's review our reflection over these first three weeks of Advent. We wait (because we don't know), we listen (because we desire Him as opposed to simply knowing about Him), and we release (because we understand that we hold ideas and grudges and sin and selfishness in our hearts).

Waiting, listening, and releasing form a pattern for how we can approach our relationship with God. This pattern of prayer humbles us, softens us, and expands our ability to see and know Him. If we are going to "prepare Him room" as a lifestyle and not simply a lyrical response for a few weeks each year, this pattern must be woven into the fabric of our lives. Henri Nouwen suggests that,

Becoming the beloved is pulling the truth revealed to me from above down into the ordinariness of what I am doing from hour to hour.

In 1 Thessalonians 5, we find a verse that is both beautiful in its simplicity and perplexing in its challenge: "pray without ceasing." The following verse says that this is God's will for us. It is His desire, His heart for us. If we see prayer as a list of requests or a duty, then this command of God sounds burdensome. However, if we see it as God's heart for us to know and experience Him throughout our day, then it is a powerful call to a different way of living. If we "know", then prayer is a chore. If we "don't know", then prayer is an adventure into life of exploring and seeing Him in all things.

Today, experiment with "unceasing prayer." Seek to stay in a place of connectedness with God. As you approach each element of your day (each conversation, each decision, each challenge), begin with simple **waiting** as you stop and acknowledge Him. Next, ask Him to speak into your situation and respond with **listening**. Finally, respond with **releasing** as you let go of self and see Him.

Sound like it might slow down your day? Then, you're getting the idea. To live in rhythm with God and His ways means slowing down. In our modern world, that sounds like quite a sacrifice and it is, but it is worth it. It is worth it because we stop missing all those moments each day when He is beautifully at work in us and through us and around us.

Begin your adventure of "prayer without ceasing" by starting with a few things each day and grow from there. Take the prayer below and put it in your own words:

Father, I admit that I am a bundle of paradoxes. I want to live in You alone. I confess this is my deepest desire and yet I have other desires. Today, give me the courage to let go. Give me the strength to repent. Give me eyes to see those places of strength to which I cling that I might release all to You. Thank you for Your patience and grace and leading in my life. Enlarge my heart. Amen.

DECEMBER 21

He Occupies Our Hearts as We Open Day 1

To receive the true gifts of Christmas, we release our hold on the gifts of this world. As we do that, we say "yes" to Christ. We welcome Him into our lives. Our hearts prepare Him room as we wait, listen, release, and now open ourselves to Him.

The Apostle John spoke of an initial receiving or opening to Christ in his Gospel.

> The true light, which enlightens everyone, was coming into the world. He was in the world, and the world was made through him, yet the world did not know him. He came to his own, and his own people did not receive him. But to **all who did receive him**, who believed in his name, he gave the right to become children of God, who were born, not of blood nor of the will of the flesh nor of the will of man, but of God. (John 1:9-13)

As we receive Him, we become children of God ... a relationship in which we are secure. However, space in our hearts and lives is cultivated only as we continue to open ourselves to Him. The Apostle John writes the words of Jesus in Revelation 3:20, "Behold, I stand at the door and knock. **If anyone hears my voice and opens the door,** I will come in to him and eat with him, and he with me."

This verse beautifully speaks of "preparing Him room." As we listen and open, we have the opportunity to experience life with Him. The tragedy is that we often don't hear that knock, but He is gracious and patient so He keeps knocking. Our lack of hearing comes because we "say, I am rich, I have prospered, and I need nothing." (Revelation 3:17) Jesus goes on to say we don't realize we "are wretched, pitiable, poor, blind, and naked."

It is our need and living in that need that opens the door of our hearts to Him. For many of us, there are perhaps those desperate times in life when we come to God out of "need" as a sort of last resort. However, we usually don't experience Him because room hasn't been prepared in our hearts. At those times, we want His gifts but on our own terms. The sense of need isn't really for Him but for our lack of those "other things." Experiencing the gift of "God with us" means that we open ourselves to Him because we are empty … we are waiting and listening and releasing … ready for Him.

Frederick Buechner describes the battle for our hearts:

> Power, success, and happiness, as the world knows them, are his who will fight for them hard enough; but peace, love, joy, are only from God. And God is the enemy whom Jacob fought there by the river, of course, and whom in one way or another we all of us fight – God, the beloved enemy. Our enemy, because, before giving us everything, he demands of us everything; before giving us life, he demands our lives – our selves, our wills, our treasure.

The verses in Revelation 3 go on to describe that God offers true riches, true worth, and true vision in the context of relationship with Him. Our great longings in life tend to be centered around lesser versions of those three things and consequently our sense of need is for material riches and earthly significance and worldly wisdom. To open ourselves to the true gifts of Christmas requires that we live with a sense of emptiness and longing for Christ Himself.

We can fool ourselves into thinking that we are releasing and letting go but still not be opening ourselves to Him. Oswald Chambers suggests,

> If a person cannot go to God, it is because he has something secret which he does not intend to give up— he may admit his sin, but would no more give up that thing than he could fly under his own power.

Are there places in your life where you readily admit your sin but **are still believing that this sin can satisfy you?** Release your belief in satisfaction in anything other than Christ and feel the emptiness. Only when we feel the emptiness of life apart from satisfaction in Him do our hearts have the space for Him to occupy. C. S. Lewis famously challenged,

> It would seem that Our Lord finds our desires not too strong, but too weak. We are half-hearted creatures, fooling about with drink and sex and ambition when infinite joy is offered us, like an ignorant child who wants to go on making mud pies in a slum because he cannot imagine what is meant by the offer of a holiday at the sea. We are far too easily pleased.

Today, set aside some time to practice the spiritual discipline of emptiness. Sit quietly and rest in Him. As your thoughts wander, bring them back to that place of rest by praying Revelation 3:17: **I am "wretched, pitiable, poor, blind, and naked" without Christ.** As you feel the "desire" of your thought system go to other things, don't try to control your thoughts but simply come back to that simple prayer. Take at least 5-10 minutes for this exercise.

Note: throughout the day, you can practice the discipline of emptiness when you feel various impulses or preoccupations by opening yourself to Him as you pray Revelation 3:17 and/or pray this prayer:

> *Father, I open myself to you. Letting go of all else, I come to you with empty, open hands. I entrust myself to You, believing that true riches, true worth, and true vision come only from You. Yes, Lord, have Your way in me. Thank You for Jesus who redeems me from the pit of self and into the joy of You. Amen.*

He Occupies Our Hearts as We Open Day 2

God the Son entered human history in the most vulnerable of ways. He didn't come with a great show of overt strength but as a baby. There is perhaps nothing more vulnerable, more fragile, more needy than a baby. He physically grew as a fetus in a young girl's womb. Such a display of poverty was not without purpose.

"For you know the grace of our Lord Jesus Christ, that though he was rich, yet for your sake he became poor, so that you by his poverty might become rich." (2 Corinthians 8:9)

Consider this: He left all His eternal glory in heaven as the second member of the Trinity to become poor. Why? So that we might be rich! So that we might move from living as vulnerable, poor, needy people into strong, unshakable people. If it is not clear at this point, Jesus is not speaking of monetary riches and poverty, although material things are not disconnected from what He is saying. In fact, as a human race, we tend to fundamentally misunderstand the concepts of poverty and wealth. It is this misunderstanding, ironically, that leaves us in a place of poverty and weakness spiritually.

We also are born into the world as poor, needy, vulnerable beings. From birth, embedded within us is a sense of need. We need some sort of stability and protection to make it through life. We *know* this intuitively. Our parents, at best, nurture and tutor us to find our strength in God, but at worst we learn an inferior and damaging way of being in the world. We learn to amass material things in order to feel strong. Indeed, we long to be "rich" but we misunderstand our true longing for "spiritual richness" found in Christ, as a longing for material riches.

In the process, the purpose of material things gets flipped. Material things were created to give a context, or a platform, for expressing spiritual realities. Part of the eternal nature of God is that He gives and receives within the Godhead. Father, Son, and Spirit are continually giving to one another. God gives to us so that we can live out that pattern of giving to others. This is the "essence of richness" … giving. However, we tend to look at material things as an opportunity to get rid of our longing to feel secure and strong. Instead of receiving and giving, we get stuck in a cycle of taking and keeping.

In Jesus' words in Revelation 3 that we might "open the door" of our hearts, he counsels those who say they are "rich." He says, you don't realize you are "poor." His counsel is simple:

> I counsel you to buy from me gold refined by fire, so that you may be rich, and white garments so that you may clothe yourself and the shame of your nakedness may not be seen, and salve to anoint your eyes, so that you may see. (Revelation 3:16-18)

Over the next three reflections, we'll look at these three items which Jesus counsels us to buy: gold refined by fire, white garments, and eye salve.

Today, gold. What is the gold that we buy from Him? First, it is significant to know that the concept of "buying" is a play on words for those who believe they are rich. God is gracious and bestows all things without cost. The metaphor would seem to be one of acquiring or obtaining. Second, the gold refined by fire is a reference to eternal, spiritual riches. Notice the description in 1 Corinthians 3:12-15:

> If any man builds on this foundation using gold, silver, costly stones, wood, hay or straw, his work will be shown for what it is, because the Day will bring it to light. It will be revealed with fire, and the fire will test the quality of each man's work. If what he has built survives, he will receive his reward. If it is burned up, he will suffer loss; he himself will be saved, but only as one escaping through the flames.

The works of man that stand God's judgment are those things which reflect His character. At the heart of God's character is the receiving and giving of love. That which we do as a reflection of His love – giving to others – is gold refined by fire! So, how do we buy that kind of gold? Consider the words of 1 Timothy 6:17-19:

> Command those who are rich in this present world not to be arrogant nor to put their hope in wealth, which is so uncertain, but to put their hope in God, who richly provides us with everything for our enjoyment. Command them to do good, to be rich in good deeds, and to be generous and

95

willing to share. In this way they will lay up treasure for themselves as a firm foundation for the coming age, so that they may take hold of the life that is truly life.

Three beautiful, challenging ideas spring from the text:

1. **Do not be arrogant.** The basic idea of arrogance is that we perceive ourselves to be the center of things. So, the idea here is simply that we join God in what He is doing rather than asking Him to join us. How often are our prayers "join me" prayers rather than "how do I join You" prayers? It may seem like a subtle distinction but it has huge ramifications.

2. **Do not put your hope in wealth.** This is the issue of our age. We believe that wealth can solve our problems. We believe that wealth can bring the stability for which we long. This is a complete inversion of the truth. The most significant issue is that material things were never created to do that. Material things can't do that. Riches might give the fleeting perception that all is well but it is fleeting at best.

3. **Be generous.** This is how we enjoy the gifts of Christmas. We take hold of the "life that is truly life" when we enact that story of "receive and give" rather than "take and keep."

Jesus came so that we might be generous to others. He came to rescue us from the prison of self where we use material things as a protection against vulnerability … where the very walls of protection become more like prison walls. How do we experience His freedom?

By joining Him in what He is doing ... letting go of the false hope of wealth ... and then giving to others.

The great spiritual writer and reformer, Teresa of Avila, wrote:
> Christ has no body now on earth but yours, no hands but yours, no feet but yours. Yours are the eyes through which Christ's compassion is to look out to the world. Yours are the feet with which Christ is to go about doing good. Yours are the hands with which Christ is to bless all people now.

This is life: to join Him, using whatever resources we have to be a part of His life. This is our invitation, our call. "Our heart must expand with all the love of heaven, to love all that God loves, to love God in all, to love with the love which God Himself gives, and whereby He makes us one with Himself." (Richard Meux Benson)

Stop and feel your neediness, your vulnerability. Consider that no amount of money can ever take away the vulnerable reality that you are hurtling through a huge universe of blackness on a tiny, little speck of dirt called earth. As you feel that, remember that our security and strength only come from joining Him in His purposes. Our lives are in His hands.

Ask God: Father, with my one life, how can I serve you today? To whom can I give today?

Make a choice to give today. Do something generous. When you do, you are opening space in your heart for Him because you are abandoning the lie that life is about you. Then, you are truly rich.

Father, I open myself to you. Letting go of all else, I come to you with empty, open hands. I entrust myself to You, believing that true riches, true worth, and true vision come only from You. Yes, Lord, have Your way in me. Thank You for Jesus who redeems me from the pit of self and into the joy of You. Amen.

He Occupies Our Hearts as We Open Day 3

As Jesus taught and ministered to others, He was misunderstood and therefore criticized routinely. One of the most prevalent critiques was for spending time with tax collectors and sinners. Interestingly, it was the theologically informed who brought these evaluations. Those who should have known the priorities of God better than anyone else viewed Jesus' priorities as being "off".

In response, Jesus said, "Those who are well have no need of a physician, but those who are sick. I came not to call the righteous, but sinners." (Mark 2:17)

Two observations about what Jesus said:

1. Jesus was not saying that some people don't have need. He was speaking tongue-in-cheek about the self-perception of the religious leaders. Clearly, the Bible teaches "no one is righteous" (Romans 3:9) in their own right. So, those who have a perception of being "well" don't have a sense of need. In other words, **there is no room in our hearts for God when we believe we've got it together.**

2. While God is always present in our lives, **we experience Him as near and enjoy His presence when we identify with our need.**

Indeed, we prepare Him room when we are aware of the void in our lives without Him. Part of this is being aware that we all have a tendency to self-righteousness. It can feel very threatening to embrace our need. It can feel shameful and embarrassing. So, we ignore evidence that we're flawed. We convince ourselves that our motives are good. We compare ourselves to others in areas where we can be self-congratulating. Whatever the means, we all have propensities toward this kind of internal dialogue.

Yesterday, we began looking at Jesus' counsel in Revelation 3 to those who have a tendency to think that they have it all together:

> I counsel you to buy from me gold refined by fire, so that you
> may be rich, and white garments so that you may clothe
> yourself and the shame of your nakedness may not be seen,
> and salve to anoint your eyes, so that you may see.
> (Revelation 3:18)

The first encouragement was to acquire gold refined by fire. This refers to the riches of doing life with Him by using our resources as a blessing to others. Space in our hearts is opened because "things" are no longer something to be possessed but something to be shared. So, they can't occupy space in our hearts.

The second encouragement is to "buy white garments so you can cover your shame." Shame is a sense that something is wrong with us and that we are unacceptable. Because we are born into sin, we inherently have a sense of shame. Whether or not we've ever identified it like that, we are embarrassed and we might even develop a harsh exterior to hide it but it is there. We feel worthless and so we attach to an image we create for ourselves.

The "white garments" are a reference to the righteousness of Christ. The idea is this: **rather than creating an image or hiding, we accept that we don't have it all together and allow Him to be the one who defines us.** Because of Christ's death on the cross, His righteousness becomes ours if we've trusted Him as our savior. When we come to know Jesus as savior, this identity is ours but we may not be living in it. The beauty of it is that we can let go of shame and rest in Him … not because we have it all together but because we are loved by Him. If we are not careful to cultivate that sense of need for Him in a balanced way, we can go back into self-righteousness. However, as we are receiving His love and acceptance, our identity moves from self to Him.

One of the most damaging images that we can attach ourselves to is "being good" or doing the "right things." There is a "goodness" that has nothing to do with God because it has everything to do with others thinking we're good. We can try to take away our own shame in this way, but it never works.

Esther de Waal, in her book *Living the Contradictions,* shared,

> This is the mystery of the Christian life, to receive a new self, which depends not on what we can achieve but on what we are willing to receive.

We do not have to attain, but simply live in the awareness of all that is ours in Christ. It is not performance but reception that is necessary. All kinds of shame can crop up in our lives during the holidays. We can feel as though there is something wrong with us. It may be a sense of loneliness or frustration over broken relationships or even the absence of relationships in our lives.

The place where shame most forcibly shows up in our lives is in whether we believe we are lovable and significant. If we live with a sense of shameful unlovableness, there is not room in our hearts for God to occupy. Neither is there room if we live with a sense of "look at me, I've got it together."

Our self-perception and performance issues will take up space where God would normally take up residence. It is God alone who can answer the question of our worth.

Henri Nouwen, in *The Inner Voice of Love*, counsels himself by saying,

> Be patient. When you feel lonely, stay with your loneliness. Avoid the temptation to let your fearful self run off. Let it teach you its wisdom; let it tell you that you can live instead of just surviving. Gradually you will become one, and you will find that Jesus is living in your heart and offering you all you need.

Do you struggle to experience the love of God in your life? Are you feeling your need and letting Him meet you there? Take a few minutes right now and ask the Lord to help you see places in your life where you are not living with a balanced sense of self. Next, let go of that self-perception and sit in the emptiness or loneliness. Finally, listen to the Lord. What does He want to tell you about who you are?

Father, I open myself to you. Letting go of all else, I come to you with empty, open hands. I entrust myself to You, believing that true riches, true worth, and true vision come only from You. Yes, Lord, have Your way in me. Thank You for Jesus who redeems me from the pit of self and into the joy of You. Amen.

He Occupies Our Hearts as We Open Day 4

As we come to the final day of the Advent Season, a line from the song "O Little Town of Bethlehem" puts things in perspective.

> Yet in thy dark streets shineth the everlasting Light. The hopes and fears of all the years are met in Thee tonight.

The hope of eternity is that we will have a living, real, vital relationship with God. Indeed, the hope is that we will have room in our hearts for God in which life makes sense in some deep, intuitive way. We want to know Him.

The fear of eternity is that we will miss out on Him and life will be a waste. We fear a meaningless existence. Whether we've ever fully been able to articulate it that way, this is our core hope and core fear. Life only makes sense in the context of relationship with God where our sense of well-being is secure, our worth is affirmed, and our vision is clear. In Jesus, the light of hope cuts through the darkness of fear. The words of John 1:4-5 develop this theme of light:

> In him was life, and the life was the light of men. The light shines in the darkness, and the darkness has not overcome it.

Clearly, in this life, we continually seek a sense of light. We look for stories that can unify and explain what is going on in life. We live our lives with a sense of story. It might be something like a national story that tells why we do what we do in a certain country. It might be a family story that says, "We do (insert some activity) because we are the (insert family name) and we are (insert some character quality)." It might be a personal sense of story of which we are only vaguely aware. It could be that we will only be happy if such and such happens in our life. It could be that things never go well for us because we just don't have what it takes to make it in this world. It could be that we will always be successful because we are better than others. Whatever the stories, we are guided by a sense of story. Stories give us a sense of light.

The challenge is that the stories we hold either affirm the one true story of the universe (our deepest hope of doing life with God) or they affirm our deepest fear (which is that we will miss out). The story of Christmas – that God injected Himself into human story so that we could do life with Him – is **the** story. It is the one story that makes sense of all things. It is the one story that gives us light. Often, it is only a sliver of light but it is the only story that rings true in our souls.

As we think back to Revelation 3 and the picture of Jesus standing at the door of our hearts, He says *open your hearts as you*,

> ...buy from me gold refined by fire, so that you may be rich, and white garments so that you may clothe yourself and the shame of your nakedness may not be seen, and salve to anoint your eyes, so that you may see. (Revelation 3:18)

The first encouragement was to acquire gold refined by fire – to pursue the riches of doing life with Him by using our resources to be a blessing to others. This opens space in our hearts as we let go of "things" as something to be possessed. The second encouragement was to clothe ourselves with His love – to allow Him to love us as we let go of shame which can also crowd our hearts.

Finally, Jesus encourages us to acquire "salve to anoint the eyes." The idea here is that we have a tendency to live by inferior stories and those stories end up darkening our vision. We may think that we are "seeing" but we keep bumping up against others. We keep stubbing our toes against our pursuits in life. Jesus offers us a story which is like salve on the eyes … it gives us the ability to see. In Matthew 6:22-24, Jesus speaks of light and story that money can make us happy:

> The eye is the lamp of the body. So, if your eye is healthy, your whole body will be full of light, but if your eye is bad, your whole body will be full of darkness. If then the light in you is darkness, how great is the darkness! No one can serve two masters, for either he will hate the one and love the other, or he will be devoted to the one and despise the other. You cannot serve God and money.

What Jesus is exposing is that we often have an affinity to stories that really just keep us in the dark. This is a danger in general and the more specific danger is that we will try to have two stories. We will try to have our own story (that we can be happy through _____) and the Christmas story. Our thinking is often that Jesus will sprinkle his magic "blessing dust" on our stories and make them work.

Author Anthony Bloom expresses the reality of the situation like this:

"We would like just one touch of heaven blue in the general picture of our life, in which there are so many dark sides ... but He is not prepared to be simply part of our life." Indeed, Jesus said, "You cannot serve God and money."

Jesus wasn't trying to be mean or petty. He was graciously stating fact: as long as we hold on to the old stories, there just simply isn't room in our hearts for His story.

Are there old perspectives and opinions and stories to which you are clinging? Are you ready to make room in your heart for the Christ story?

Helen Keller, a remarkable woman who also happened to be blind, said, "The only thing worse than being blind is having sight but no vision." She was also asked, "Isn't it terrible to be blind?" She replied, "It is better to be blind and see with your heart than to have two eyes and see nothing."

We apply the salve to our eyes as we walk by faith rather than by sight (2 Corinthians 5:7). In this context, sight is looking with our natural eyes ... allowing the lenses of earthly stories to interpret what we see. Faith is looking at life with His eyes ... allowing His story to interpret and define what we see.

In 2 Corinthians 4:16-18, the Apostle Paul writes,

> So we do not lose heart. Though our outer self is wasting away, our inner self is being renewed day by day. For this light momentary affliction is preparing for us an eternal

weight of glory beyond all comparison, as we look not to the things that are seen but to the things that are unseen. For the things that are seen are transient, but the things that are unseen are eternal.

The glory of beginning to see with His eyes is that we begin to see Him everywhere. We begin to connect the dots and see that He has been present all along. He is at work in us. He is weaving together a story that we won't fully see until eternity but the beauty is that His life, His presence, in the midst of it all, is the story. That is the light! Seeing Him and knowing that He is near is all we need. At times, we might claim that we want more but He alone is truly sufficient – satisfying – to our souls. It can be a bit terrifying to let go of old stories … those narratives which seem to give us a sense of comfort.

A. W. Tozer said,

> Hardly anything else reveals so well the fear and uncertainty among men as the length to which they will go to hide their true selves from each other and even from their own eyes. Almost all men live from childhood to death with a semiopaque curtain, coming out briefly only when forced by some emotional shock and then retreating as quickly as possible into hiding again.… Self-knowledge is so critically important to us in our pursuit of God and His righteousness that we lie under heavy obligation to do immediately whatever is necessary to remove the disguise and permit our real selves to be known.

As a final step in preparing room in your heart, take a few minutes today and ask the Father for some self-knowledge. Is there a "story" that you've been using to light your way that is not part of God's story? Is there a story that you need to release today? Pay attention to anxiety, anger, fear, and shame. If you notice them, ask God to show you a story you might release. Stand blind before Him, putting all your "lights" down. Let go of all else and ask Him for faith to see with His light. His light is simple: God with us. Nothing more, nothing less. His presence is all we need. Be attentive to His presence today by simply reminding your heart: God is with me.

Father, I open myself to you. Letting go of all else, I come to you with empty, open hands. I entrust myself to You, believing that true riches, true worth, and true vision come only from You. Yes, Lord, have Your way in me. Thank You for Jesus who redeems me from the pit of self and into the joy of You. Amen.

We celebrate Him as
He occupies our hearts

"God longs for a temple, not of stone and light, but of flesh and blood and a heart of full of love. Like Mary, you are God's temple, for when you say 'yes' to God you open yourself to God and God's glory abides in you; when you say 'yes' to God, the Word is made flesh and dwells among us." (James Koester)

We can say "yes" to God with confidence and trust because He has already said "yes" to us.

> For all the promises of God find their Yes in him. That is why it is through him that we utter our Amen to God for his glory. (2 Corinthians 1:20)

All of His promises center around one strong, glorious, satisfying truth: "I will never leave you or forsake you." In Jesus, God is with us. Ultimately, this is what can open our hearts to experiencing Him and knowing Him in every ounce of life. Because He is with us, there is no joy or hurt or "boring" detail in which He is not present.

Today, simply celebrate Immanuel, "God with us," by remembering that He is present. His presence means that all things can be viewed as a gift through which He can be known and enjoyed.

When I enjoy family and friends, I am reminded that He is my Father and true friend.

When I open a gift, I am reminded that He is the "Son that was given."

When I am in pain, I am reminded that He alone is my joy.

When I am suffering unjustly, I am reminded that He is my justice.

When I am lonely, I am reminded that I am never alone.

When I am eating a meal, I am reminded Jesus is the bread of life.

When I am (fill in the blank), I am reminded that all is a gift.

C. S. Lewis put this in beautiful perspective, "The great thing, if one can, is to stop regarding all the unpleasant things as interruptions of one's 'own' or 'real' life. The truth is of course that what one calls the interruptions are precisely one's real life -- the life God is sending one, day by day."

Hold this prayer before God all day today: *All is gift. Thank you, Father.* Bring your heart and mind back to this simple prayer all day long.

DISCUSSION GUIDE

If you have a desire to discuss and share how God is at work in you through these days of Advent, here are a few suggestions for how you might structure a time of discussion and sharing.

1. Daily Discussion with friends and/or family: select a question from the day's devotional and share how you answered the question. Pray the daily prayer together.

2. Weekly Discussion:
   a. Review the theme of the week and how the theme relates to preparing room in your heart.
   b. Share how you have been challenged by the theme of the week.
   c. Discuss a scripture passage or concept that you found particularly insightful or helpful.
   d. Share one way that you will engage your "life with God" differently this week.
   e. Pray for one another.
   f. Pray the weekly prayer together.

ABOUT THE AUTHOR

Dr. Ted Wueste

Ted lives in Phoenix with his wife and two children. After serving nine years as the Senior Pastor of a church he planted, he now serves as Executive Pastor of Spiritual Formation in a large evangelical church in Phoenix. In addition, Ted offers spiritual direction and spends time co-directing the *Spiritual Formation Society of Arizona* – a network and support to those involved in spiritual formation ministry. He holds an M.Div. from Western Seminary and an STM from Dallas Seminary as well as Doctor of Ministry in Leadership from Phoenix Seminary. Ted also serves as an adjunct professor in Spiritual Formation at Phoenix Seminary.

For more information about Ted's spiritual direction ministry, you can go to desertdirection.com where he also blogs regularly.

Made in the USA
San Bernardino, CA
08 December 2018